BIRDS IN NEST BOXES

How to Help, Study, and Enjoy Birds When Snags Are Scarce

By Charlotte C. Corkran

Char Corkran

D1562944

Photographs by
Beverly A. LaBelle and the author

Publication of this book, and related research, were supported by grants and contributions from: Northwest Ecological Research Institute, Erick Campbell, Mazamas Research Committee, Oregon Parks Foundation, Oregon Wildlife Heritage Foundation, Sierra Club Foundation, Bluebird Recovery Program of the Audubon Chapter of Minneapolis, Oregon Chapter of the Wildlife Society, North American Bluebird Society, Mt. Hood National Forest, and PhotoCraft.

Naturegraph Publishers, Inc.

Library of Congress Cataloging-in-Publication Data
Corkran, Charlotte C., 1945-
  Birds in nest boxes : how to help, study, and enjoy birds when
snags are scarce/by Charlotte C. Corkran; photographs by
Beverly A. LaBelle and the author.-- 1st ed.
    p. cm.
  Includes bibliographical references (p.).
  ISBN 0-87961-270-3
  1. Birdhouses. 2. Birds--Nests. I. LaBelle, Beverly A., ill. II.
Title.
  QL676.5.C555.2004
  639.9'78--dc22

                        2004003593

Cover design by
Charlotte C. Corkran and Beverly A. LaBelle

Cover photos: White-breasted Nuthatches (LaBelle), Western Red Cedar
snag with old woodpecker hole. Back cover: Students checking chickadee
nest box (LaBelle).

Naturegraph Publishers has been publishing books on
natural history, Native Americans, and outdoor subjects since
1946. Please write for our free catalog.

Books for a better world

Naturegraph Publishers, Inc.
PO Box 1047 ● 3543 Indian Creek Rd.
Happy Camp, CA 96039
(530) 493-5353
www.naturegraph.com

CONTENTS

ACKNOWLEDGMENTS

The Northwest Ecological Research Institute (NERI) is a group of wonderfully generous people, and I have received the full benefits of their knowledge, support, and tireless work since we started the organization in 1984. Philip Gaddis was the founder of NERI and the project leader for the chickadee and bluebird studies. I will be indebted to him forever for letting me tag along, learn from his wealth of wildlife wisdom, gain the confidence to do my own wildlife work, and finally inherit his bluebird project. Ginny Taylor spent months of her life with me over the years, sharing the fun of checking nest boxes on every project. Hal Hushbeck made all phases of the bluebird study both better and more enjoyable, including field work, literature review, and study analysis. Dave Fouts graciously provided information from his years of incredible dedication to Purple Martins. Mirth Walker reviewed the first draft and gave me much needed encouragement. Bev LaBelle and other NERI members, including Teresa DeLorenzo, Paul Dickinson, Cathy Flick, Karl Hartzell, Eve Heidtmann, Gayle Joiner, Donna Lusthoff, and Chena Weitzer checked many nest boxes and helped pull all the data together. Thanks also to a whole bunch of other Wetland Wildlife Watch and bluebird volunteers, Dave Corkran, and students from the Catlin Gabel School.

A number of individuals in several agencies have been outstandingly helpful over the years. Foremost is Rick Kneeland, previously a wildlife biologist for the Mt. Hood National Forest (NF), whose enthusiasm and creativity in project design gave me my first opportunities as a wildlife consultant and therefore launched my career. Barb Kott, Maggie Gould, Carol Hughes, Wendy Evans, Alan Dyck, and Leslie HaySmith from the Mt. Hood NF kept Wetland Wildlife Watch gathering data used in this manual. Steve Allen and Greg Hattan from the Oregon Department of Fish and Wildlife, and Scott Cooke and Dick Cosgriffe from the U. S. Bureau of Land Management have been facilitators and information sources for our bluebird study sites at the Phil Schneider Wildlife Management Area.

I deeply appreciate the private landowners around Fossil, Oregon, who have cheerfully allowed us to continue the bluebird study for so many years. Brian Sharp initiated the study when he worked for the U. S. Fish and Wildlife Service, and has allowed us to use his property as our home base there. John and Jean Rumble and Lois Hunt have always made us feel welcome, and Rick Stanley has been very gracious. Here's to the memory of Pete Campbell, Alvie Hunt, Jack Steiwer, and Bill Steiwer, four wonderful gentlemen who passed away during these years. Heartfelt thanks also to Ada Ruth and Lawrence Whitmore and family, as well as the other private landowners around Bickleton, Washington, for all the great weekends checking nest boxes and staying at the Whoop-N-Holler Ranch and Museum.

Many individuals helped us find nests to photograph and gave us their insights about and experiences with particular species. My thanks to Vicki Arthur, Glen Bauer, Muffin Burgess, Dave Flaming, Rhoda Fleischman and Shannon Duffy, Chris Dwyer, Cathy Flick, Dave Fouts, Diane Gadway, Linda Hale, Bill Haight, Stewart and Debby Janes, Pat Johnston, Stewart Johnston, Stan Kostka, Kevin Li, Dianne MacRae, Donna Mauch and Deb Shaffer, Don and Carol McCartney, Roger Orness, Myrna Pearman, Mark Prchal, Kathy and Dave Rogers, Howard and Elaine Sands, Harvey Tucker and Linda Hoagland, Mike and Christopher Uhtoff, Dan Varland, Patty Vaughan and students from the Forks Alternative School, and Dennis Vroman.

I am especially grateful to those who reviewed the draft and otherwise made such valuable suggestions for improvements, including Bob Altman, Cathy Flick, Dave Fouts, Karl Hartzell, Hal Hushbeck, Robert Marheine, Betty Shadoan, Jack Remington, Ginny Taylor, and Dan Varland. Thanks also to Casey Huff and students at California State University, Chico, for editing the manuscript.

I truly appreciate the grants that have enabled this and related projects to keep going. Erick Campbell of the Bureau of Land Management, the Mazamas Research Committee, the Oregon Parks Foundation, the North American Bluebird Society, the Bluebird Recovery Program of the Audubon Chapter of Minneapolis, the Mt. Hood NF, and the board of NERI have been both generous and patient. Publication of this book has been supported by grants from the Oregon Wildlife Heritage Foundation, the Sierra Club Foundation, the Oregon Chapter of The Wildlife Society, and NERI, for which I am very grateful.

Although the majority of this manual is based on my own experiences and those of other NERI members, I also made extensive use of several published works to inform, substantiate, and increase the region of inference of our data. These included California Waterfowl Association (1994), Ehrlich et al. (1988), Harrison (1978), Henderson (1992), Link (1999), Pearman (2002), Scriven (1989), Sheldon (1998), D. and L. Stokes (1990), Tuttle and Hensley (2001), and information leaflets from the North American Bluebird Society and the Bluebird Recovery Program of the Audubon Chapter of Minneapolis. Complete bibliographic information is provided in the References at the end of this book.

During incubation, a female Wood Duck leaves her eggs twice a day to feed. The down feathers that she plucked from her belly keep the eggs warm while she is away. Some of the down falls through holes or cracks in the nest box.   LaBelle

INTRODUCTION

Looking into nest boxes is just like opening Christmas presents. Every box could contain an exquisitely crafted nest, jewel-like eggs, or the brave beauty of an incubating bird. Since 1984, I have been peering into nest boxes on a regular basis. It started with research on chickadees in areas where gypsy moths were being eradicated using a biological control agent. Then I began monitoring wildlife using nest boxes on national forest lands. A study of bluebirds where pesticide application for grasshopper control was planned gradually turned into a study of bluebird productivity in different grassland types. It has become a habit now, or perhaps an addiction. Nest boxes just have to be opened.

What a lost opportunity it seems when someone takes the time to build a nest box and nail it onto a tree but never goes back to see what kind of wildlife uses it. Examining the layers of evidence to figure out what happened in a box is in-

Bluebird eggs in a nest of grass with a juniper bark lining.   LaBelle

9

triguing detective work. I hope this book will inspire kids and adults alike, classes of students and groups of retirees, to get involved in the fascinating work of nest box monitoring.

Monitoring bird populations is becoming an increasingly important activity among biologists and amateur birdwatchers. Several bird species that use nest boxes are Neotropical migrants, that is, birds that breed in North America but spend the winters in Central or South America. An international group called Partners in Flight recognizes the importance of monitoring populations of both Neotropical migrants and resident species, and is trying to standardize the gathering of data. Different methods of data collection work best with different groups of birds. For the species that nest in cavities but generally do not excavate their own, checking a group of nest boxes is by far the most effective method of population monitoring. This book provides both the information and the protocol for monitoring these secondary cavity nesting birds.

The primary focus of this book is on the bird species that are always or typically secondary cavity nesters. However, if you monitor many of their nests you will run into some rodents, and probably several other creatures, so the evidence of other commonly found inhabitants is also described. Besides, the flying squirrels, bumblebees, and other native wildlife need our help, too. The field work and photography for this book occurred in Oregon and Washington; however, the information and monitoring protocol are applicable in much of the western United States and Canada, at least anywhere there are trees (the cactus dwelling specialists are not covered).

SNAGS

A snag is a tree that has died yet remains standing upright. But it is so much more. It is the link between the past forest generation and the future one. It is still important in modifying the atmosphere, by storing carbon, slowing the release of carbon dioxide that was gathered by the living tree (Aber et al. 2001). As it breaks down by decay and erosion, it is a cornucopia of nutrients ready to be added to the soil (Franklin et al. 1981). And it is home for multitudes of living things, from bacteria to beetles to bluebirds to bears.

In an undisturbed old-growth forest in the Pacific Northwest, snags are usually numerous. After a stand-replacing wildfire, of course, there may be scores of snags per acre. As a new forest generation begins, they tower over the seedling trees. Eventually, one by one, wind and decay bring them down. As the younger forest matures, fewer large snags remain, but competition and other factors continually cull out individual trees that become small and medium-sized snags. After many years the forest has large trees again, that become large snags when they die. The conventional view of a perfect forest cycle is instruc-

Snag with holes where woodpeckers have been feeding on insects.   LaBelle

11

A GENERALIZED FOREST CYCLE

CLOCKWISE FROM BELOW: young forest, Bobcat, old-growth forest, Northern Spotted Owl, forest fire,

burned snags, wood boring
beetle larva (LaBelle),
Northern Flicker male,
Mountain Bluebird male,
down log (LaBelle), Western
Red-backed Salamander.

tive but far less interesting than the chaotic complexity of reality (Rapp 2003). At any stage in the cycle, disease, wind, small fires, and extreme weather can break up the homogeneous cohort of trees that we call a stand, creating patches of snags and small openings where new trees begin again.

Some snags crumble gradually from the top, creating vast debris mounds around the snags' bases. Others weaken at the base and topple suddenly, transforming into logs. In either case, they enter into the third and final phase of the trees' useful role in the forest ecosystem. Each tree provides more habitat niches, supports more species, and lasts longer once it dies than it did when it was alive (Franklin et al. 1981, Maser and Trappe 1984, Maser et al. 1984). From the standpoint of wildlife, the cycle of living tree to standing snag to down log or debris mound is the key to species diversity.

But snags and their diverse dependents are in trouble. Why have snags become scarce? There are different reasons in different areas. For instance, until recently most forest managers did not know the importance of snags. In the United States, worker safety regulations for most logging systems required snags to be cut down because they were dangerous and might fall on loggers. Also, snags stood in the way of fast-growing young trees. Now, with new information and modified public priorities, National Forest timber sale planners are providing protection for snags either individually or in undisturbed patches, and creating snags where they are infrequent. However, years of cutting them down have left vast landscapes with no large dead trees. Management practices have not yet changed in many private, state, and provincial forests. In managed forests, trees still are not allowed to grow large enough to be the most useful in the ecosystem. And look around your city or town. How many snags can you find? Most people do not realize the value of dead trees but instead consider them unsightly and hazardous. Snags are cut down and replaced with young living trees, (or with utility poles, street lights, and road signs.) Even in natural area parks, dead and dying trees are cut down. Certainly there is a hazard if a snag looms over a home or a picnic table. But there has been little recognition of the important roles that snags play in many ecosystems, and little tolerance for leaving them to fulfill those roles.

What can be done to solve the complex problem of snag scarcity? We must consider both long-term and short-term solutions. In the grand scheme of things, we must grow huge trees and let some of them die. That will mean producing timber on a 300- or 400-year rotation. But even the most optimistic environmentalist would have to admit that long rotation tree harvesting is unlikely to occur on many acres of public or private forests. And what about farmlands, industrial areas, cities, and suburban landscapes that once were wooded or grew scattered large trees? While growing, retaining, and creating snags are increasing on commercial forest land, and must be encouraged at least in suburban areas and parks, snag habitat in the western United States and Canada will be severely limited for the foreseeable future.

Even if we start now growing large trees for the future, it will take many years. Some of the wildlife species dependent on snags cannot wait. In the interim, nest boxes are probably the best solution. Preferably made from scrap and recycled wood or sections of small logs, nest boxes are easy to build and provide nesting sites for most secondary cavity nesting birds. They are also the easiest tool for monitoring popula-

Downy Woodpeckers can use very small snags if there are no large ones.   LaBelle

Western Bluebird female at a nest box.   LaBelle

tions of these species. Furthermore, nest boxes can be a tool for reintroducing species that have been lost or decreased in local areas. As an example, the White-breasted Nuthatch has disappeared from the Puget Sound area in Washington, along with its favored oak woodlands. Perhaps nest boxes could be put up where replacement oaks are slowly growing. Then young nuthatches raised in nest boxes elsewhere could be captured and released into the new habitat, where they would readily use the new nest boxes. Both the Western Bluebird and the Purple Martin have been brought back to many parts of this region by the efforts of dedicated individuals using boxes and gourds to provide nesting sites. These success stories are documented in many publications, including Fouts (1996) and Keyser (2002).

However, nest boxes should be just one small part of a broader plan for protecting and managing habitat for native wildlife. Nest boxes imitate only one of the features of snags – sheltered cavities for nesting and resting – and do not replace the foraging habitat for wildlife or the other critical functions of snags. Providing appropriate, year-round food sources, water, and shelter from weather and predators are just as important as providing boxes for nesting cavities. Where boxes completely replace snags, the natural community of bird species can be skewed, and the long-term survival of even the secondary cavity nesting species becomes tenuous.

So, for the time being we must protect snags wherever possible, create some snags and cavities, and provide some nest boxes elsewhere. We must teach people to accept a little of the messiness in nature, and to appreciate dead trees for their beauty, their importance to wildlife, and their central role in nutrient storage and cycling. The short-term solutions to the scarcity of snags are easy and enjoyable, especially the use of nest boxes. The long-term solutions will require all of us to be farsighted, generous, and committed.

CAVITY NESTING

When you think about it, nesting in a hole within a snag is such a good idea it is a wonder any birds build their nests out on a branch. The thick wood of the trunk is excellent insulation, keeping the nest warm in cold weather and cool in the heat of summer. It provides sure protection from the wind and rain (although some cavities collect water running down the trunk). Brown-headed Cowbirds, that parasitize other species by laying eggs in their nests, only rarely use cavities as egg-laying sites. Predators may not notice a nest concealed in a cavity, although many can enter or reach into it if they do notice it.

Ash-throated Flycatcher in an old woodpecker hole.   LaBelle

EARTH CAVITY USERS

CAVE OR ROCK	BURROW IN SOIL
Pelagic Cormorant	+ Fork-tailed Storm-Petrel
Red-breasted Merganser	+ Leach's Storm-Petrel
Turkey Vulture	+ Ancient Murrelet
Prairie Falcon	+ Cassin's Auklet
Peregrine Falcon	Rhinoceros Auklet
Pigeon Guillemot	+ Tufted Puffin
Black Swift	+ Horned Puffin
White-throated Swift	Burrowing Owl
Black Phoebe	- Belted Kingfisher
- Say's Phoebe	N. Rough-winged Swallow
-* Violet-green Swallow	Bank Swallow
Rock Wren	
Canyon Wren	- Also uses tree cavities
American Dipper	* Also uses cavities created
Townsend's Solitaire	by woodpeckers
American Pipit	+ Also uses rock cavities
Gray-crowned Rosy-Finch	
Black Rosy-Finch	

Not every cavity that birds use for nesting is a woodpecker hole. Some types of cavities are not even in trees. Varied species such as Belted Kingfishers and Tufted Puffins nest in burrows in the ground. Peregrine Falcons, American Dippers, and many others use caves or rock cavities. Cliff Swallows create their own cavities, using bill-fulls of mud to build the walls.

Trees, particularly the venerable giant snags and living old growth trees, produce several types of nooks and crannies that birds can use directly. Vaux's Swifts make use of the hollow trunks of broken-topped snags, or those split open by lightning. Brown Creepers (as well as many bats) use the crevice formed when a slab of bark partially separates from the trunk, creating a lean-to shelter. The wound where a branch broke off may be invaded by fungi and other decay organisms. The wood inside the wound may soften to the point where a Black-capped Chickadee can dig out a small nest hole without relying on a woodpecker to do the work. A larger wound may rot out a cavity suitable in size for a Common Merganser or a Barn Owl. Even a treetop less than a foot in diameter can provide a crevice for a bluebird if it breaks off and lands in a horizontal position with a jagged space at the break.

TREE CAVITY USERS

NON-WOODPECKER HOLLOWS OR CREVICES

* Common Merganser	(Steller's Jay)
+ (Merlin)	Brown Creeper
+ Barn Owl	Winter Wren
+ Great Horned Owl	(Song Sparrow)
Northern Spotted Owl	(Dark-eyed Junco)
Barred Owl	(Brewer's Blackbird)
* Vaux's Swift	(House Finch)
*+ Western Flycatcher	

      *   Also uses cavities created by woodpeckers

      +   Also uses rock cavities

      ( )   Rarely uses cavities

But woodpeckers, the primary excavators, are the champion agents for transforming a tree trunk into an apartment complex. Many do not wait for the tree to completely die, but carve an entrance hole through the living sapwood and excavate the nest chamber in rotting heartwood (Hildebrand and Parks 2002). The size of the cavity varies, of course, with the size of the excavator. According to Harrison (1978), the

Brown Creeper emerging from its nest under a loose slab of bark on an oak snag.

Downy Woodpecker nest cavity from outside, and split showing inside. LaBelle

Downy Woodpecker's entrance hole is about 3 cm. (1¼ in.) in diameter, and the nest chamber can be only 6 cm. (2½ in.) in diameter and 20 cm. (8 in.) deep. At the other extreme, the Pileated Woodpecker's entrance hole is about 10 cm. (4 in.), and the nest chamber is often 20 by 60 cm. (8 by 24 in.). Most woodpecker pairs bore out a new nest hole every year, rather than reusing them. Individual woodpeckers carve out additional cavities for roosting at night. With plenty of snags and several species of woodpeckers, a forest may have cavities to spare. However, competition for those spare rooms can be fierce.

In the western United States and Canada, excluding southern desert cactus-dwellers, there are 31 bird species that rely on or frequently nest in chambers hollowed out by other birds. If you add the primary excavators and those that commonly use other crevices and hollows in trees, there are 52 native species of birds, about 17 percent of all the native bird species that breed in this region, competing for nesting space inside trees and snags (Harrison 1978, Ehrlich et al. 1988). The birds are joined by pine marten, rodents, bats, bees, beetles, ants, and assorted other vertebrates and invertebrates. If you add up all the species of just the vertebrates that regularly nest, hide, rest, store food, or search for food in or on snags, you arrive at about 25 percent of the birds, and 22 percent of all the vertebrate wildlife (not including fish) of the region – and a realization of the critical importance of snags (Brown 1985, Puchy and Marshall 1993).

PRIMARY EXCAVATORS

TREE CAVITIES CREATED FOR OWN USE

* Lewis' Woodpecker	White-headed Woodpecker
Acorn Woodpecker	Three-toed Woodpecker
Yellow-bellied Sapsucker	Black-backed Woodpecker
Red-naped Sapsucker	* Northern Flicker
Red-breasted Sapsucker	Pileated Woodpecker
Williamson's Sapsucker	* Black-capped Chickadee
Nuttall's Woodpecker	* Chestnut-backed Chickadee
Downy Woodpecker	*- Red-breasted Nuthatch
Hairy Woodpecker	* Pygmy Nuthatch

    *   Also uses cavities created by (other) woodpeckers
    -    Also uses tree cavities

SECONDARY CAVITY USERS

CAVITIES CREATED BY OTHER SPECIES

- Wood Duck	- Ash-throated Flycatcher
- Common Goldeneye	Purple Martin
- Barrow's Goldeneye	- Tree Swallow
- Bufflehead	- Mountain Chickadee
- Hooded Merganser	- Boreal Chickadee
- American Kestrel	- Oak Titmouse
- Flammulated Owl	- Juniper Titmouse
- Western Screech-Owl	**-White-breasted Nuthatch
- Northern Hawk Owl	- Bewick's Wren
- Northern Pygmy-Owl	+- House Wren
- Boreal Owl	Western Bluebird
- Northern Saw-whet Owl	+ Mountain Bluebird

    **   Also creates its own cavities
    -    Also uses tree cavities
    +   Also uses rock cavities

PRIMARY EXCAVATORS. Top: Hairy Woodpecker female with an insect for her nestlings. Lower left: Lewis' Woodpecker delivering food to its nestlings (LaBelle), Lower right: Red-breasted Nuthatches usually make their own nest cavities, but sometimes use other holes or a nest box (LaBelle).

SECONDARY CAVITY NESTERS

The term "secondary cavity nesting" is used to describe both those species that use chambers previously excavated by woodpeckers as well as those that use existing holes and crevices in trees, soil, or rock. Among the birds, these species are not all related, but include members of several families. They come from the ranks of waterfowl, raptors (hawks and owls), swallows, chickadees, thrushes, and others. Rarely, they include several bird species that usually nest elsewhere, including other raptors, a jay, and several members of the sparrow and finch tribes. Why should we be concerned about this artificial and disparate grouping of bird species? There are at least four reasons.

First, this group of birds is composed of beautiful, intriguing, and valuable wildlife. Most of us derive great pleasure from watching a kestrel hovering over a field or a nuthatch upside-down poking under the bark of a tree. The group includes important predators of rodents and insects that would harm native plant communities and agricultural crops alike if their populations were not maintained in some kind of harmony with their habitats. The smaller members are a particularly important part of the food base for native predators.

Barrow's Goldeneye male.

Second, snags are less numerous now because urban and suburban developments have taken over so many acres of forest land in our region, and because intensive timber management has not retained snags until recently. Fewer snags mean fewer woodpeckers and even fewer cavities for nesting. The number of available cavities can be the single factor most responsible for limiting the population of these species in any given area (Thomas 1979). When competition for cavities increases, the birds may expend more energy fighting for homes than raising their young, and may destroy each others' eggs and nestlings in their efforts to claim a nest site.

Third, those fewer cavities are frequently usurped by two species introduced here from other countries, namely the European Starling and the House Sparrow (or English Sparrow). Both are aggressive, adaptable, and prolific. They are associated with habitats disturbed by humans. Anywhere near cities, towns, and farms these two invaders regularly outcompete the native species. If left uncontrolled, the population of starlings in particular can reach staggering numbers. The damage to native wildlife caused by these exotic species can hardly be exaggerated.

Violet-green Swallow female at a weathered nest box.   LaBelle

SECONDARY CAVITY NESTERS. Top: A Hooded Merganser male raises his crest during courtship. Lower left: Northern Pygmy-Owls are sometimes seen in the daytime during their nesting season. Lower right: Male Western Bluebird, a species that has made a comeback because of nest boxes (LaBelle).

Fourth, several of the secondary cavity nesting species that breed in this region are Neotropical migrants, meaning that they fly to the New World tropics (in Central and South America) to spend the months during our winters. The two long flights a year are full of hazards, but so are the winter months. Tropical forests are being cut down much faster than those in North America, and generally they are not replaced.

Chemical insecticides and herbicides long since banned in the United States and Canada are still commonly used in the developing countries, causing deaths or health problems to birds – as well as to humans.

Several resident species and a few of those that fly here from the tropics and nest in snag cavities appear to be experiencing population declines (Partners in Flight website, Sharp 1996). The trends for many other secondary cavity nesting species are simply not known. Only by a concerted and widespread program to monitor their populations will we be able to document problems and track responses to our efforts to help this fascinating group of birds.

European Starling at a cavity in a snag.   LaBelle

STAGES OF THE NESTING CYCLE

As with every other facet in the study of birds, the beauty of the nesting cycle is in the details, and in the diversity of species' styles. However, it is convenient to generalize and name some of the phases when examining nests and recording notes. The reproductive cycle of birds is most easily considered as a series of discrete stages: courtship, nest site selection, nest construction, fertilization and egg laying, incubation, egg hatching, growth and development of chicks, fledging, and separation from the parents. Several of these stages may overlap, be shortened or lengthened or skipped in certain species, and be repeated with second and third broods. Bird courtship and the other behavioral stages of the breeding cycle are eloquently discussed in several other books and are beyond the scope of this manual. Nest site selection is discussed starting on page 41. The stages that are expressed in terms of the nest, eggs, or chicks that you might find in a cavity or nest box are treated here. For further information, see Baicich and Harrison (1997), Berger et al. (2001), Ehrlich et al. (1988), Harrison (1978), and Pearman (2002), which were used in the preparation of this chapter.

Chestnut-backed Chickadee nestling (early Stage V).

Red-breasted Nuthatch scattering wood chips while excavating a nest cavity.   LaBelle

NEST CONSTRUCTION

Even if you never watch a bird building its nest, you need only examine an old nest to appreciate the bird's incredible dexterity. Relying on its bill as the primary tool, the bird collects, prepares, carries, and organizes materials into an efficient temporary home. Exceptions are Ospreys and eagles which use their feet to break off and carry sticks, and then use their bills to arrange them into a nest. Of course, many birds, including nighthawks and most shorebirds, build no nest at all. Woodpeckers excavate a nest cavity but carry the wood chips out and lay their eggs on the bare floor. Cavity nesting ducks and kestrels bring no materials in to the nest site, although the ducks pull out their own belly feathers and down to cover the eggs. Owls bring nothing or a few food items to cache around the nest, or they may regurgitate pellets of undigested food.

Most songbirds do construct nests, and it is helpful to divide that construction process into the following phases:

1. bracing or attaching the nest start
2. building the nest base
3. forming walls around a cup
4. lining the cup

Even if a nest is abandoned before it is completed, by looking at the type of construction it is often possible to determine which species began the nesting process (see page 111).

The secondary cavity nesters skip the first phase altogether, because they do not need to build a platform to brace the nest across branches, or weave the attachment to the branches. The natural cavity or nest box provides the firm and secure foundation.

The second phase, building the nest base, is highly variable among the different species of secondary cavity nesters. However, most species groups have a characteristic material that they accumulate in the cavity to form the base of the nest. Swallows usually bring in long pieces of grasses, while chicka-dees collect wads of moss. Blue-

Western Flycatcher's woven nest attached in a pine sapling.

birds often skip this second phase altogether. Not as much energy is spent in arranging the nest base as in bringing in the materials, because its functions are merely to provide insulation and to support the nest cup. When the cavity is a nest box, the base is square in shape to fill in the corners.

The third phase, forming walls around a cup, can be accomplished in two ways, either down or up. The bird may push down into the nest base while pulling or tweaking at the materials and turning around repeatedly to form a cup around its body. Alternatively, the bird may build the walls up, bringing in materials specifically for the walls. The first sign of a bluebird nest may be a circle or cylinder of grass with the bare floor of the cavity showing in the middle. Pushing, pulling, weaving, and rotating its body, the bird erects walls around itself that will protect and insulate the eggs and nestlings while not collapsing in on them. Chickadees and nuthatches may push the cup down into the base, but then they build up a fluffy mass around the top, which they

Left: Mountain Chickadee nest with coverlet in place, right: with coverlet pulled open to show the eggs.

use as a coverlet, pulling it over the eggs whenever they leave the nest.

The fourth phase is lining the cup. The bird brings in additional materials, specifically the softest and warmest materials, and weaves or places them around inside the cup. Feathers of just the right size and curve are used, or hair that can be wound around in a circle. This phase is often skipped by bluebirds and by smaller species if the walls of the nest are built of a material that is particularly soft and warm. David Winkler (1993) has found that the large feathers lining and arching over Tree Swallow nests significantly speed up the nestlings' early growth. Occasionally, a bird adds a final touch that appears more decorative than functional, but may startle or distract a potential predator. Pieces of shed snakeskin are a frequent addition to Bewick's Wren nests, and the urban alternative is small cellophane wrappers. Whether plain or fancy, the final nest cup is both cushy and strong, and it is precisely the right width and depth for the female's body to fill in order to hold her precious heat against the eggs.

An exception to the secondary cavity nesters in all aspects of nest building is the Vaux's Swift. It builds a tiny platform cup of twigs glued to the inside of a large cavity using special saliva. That simple platform is the brace, the base, and the walls. No lining is used. The fragile structure barely holds the female and eggs or hatchlings. Before their eyes open, the nestlings are capable of clambering around on the rough walls of the snag (or chimney), using their outsized feet with each of the four toes clinging from a different direction.

EGG LAYING

Generally, the eggs are laid one per day until the clutch is complete. Hooded Mergansers and some of the small owls lay an egg every other day. During the egg laying phase, unless incubation begins with the first egg, the parents stay out of the nest except for the female's visit to lay each egg.

Occasionally, one egg is very small and never hatches; it is likely the first egg laid by a young bird in its first breeding season. Young birds are also more apt to abandon their eggs if disturbed while laying eggs or before they have really settled into incubating them.

INCUBATION

Two strategies are apparent in the incubation of eggs. Either the bird starts incubating as soon as the first one or two eggs are laid, or it waits until most or all of the clutch has been laid. In the first instance, eggs hatch one at a time,

Western
Screech-Owl
incubating
eggs in a
nest box.

resulting in chicks of different ages. This strategy is efficient if food resources may be scarce. The oldest chicks will dominate in begging for food, so at least some of the chicks are likely to receive enough to survive. Furthermore, by reducing the time to hatching for the first eggs laid, the parent birds can take advantage of a brief but rich food source. Finally, decreasing the number of days in the nest limits the opportunities for predation on the earliest chicks. Among the secondary cavity nesters, only owls and kestrels follow this strategy. The others, both ducks and songbirds, lay the full clutch of eggs before beginning to incubate them, so they all hatch at about the same time. This strategy is efficient at producing the most offspring when food is plentiful, but occasionally leads to abandonment of nests if there is a drastic food shortage.

In most species only the female incubates the eggs while the male often provides food. Male kestrels and chickadees may help with the incubating. For the first few days of incubation, the eggs can survive chilling. Once the development process has really begun, the eggs must be kept constantly warm by the parent's body. An area on the belly of the bird loses its feathers (female ducks pluck out their own feathers and down) and develops additional capillaries next to the skin to increase heat transfer to the eggs. The eggs of the larger ducks and raptors require about a month of incubation, while those of the smaller songbirds hatch in about two weeks.

American Kestrel male delivering food to its nestlings.   LaBelle

EGG HATCHING

It seems impossible that the tiny chick, packed tightly inside its egg, can move sufficiently to peck open the shell and emerge. The process of hatching may take many hours, with plenty of time-outs for resting, particularly in larger species with sturdy shells, like ducks. The parent continues to incubate during hatching, and often the parent and chicks communicate vocally. Soon after the chicks have hatched, the parents eat the eggshells or carry them out of the nest.

The hatching time is a vulnerable period. A disturbance that causes the parent to leave the nest may permit the chicks to die before fully hatching. Either the chicks become chilled, or they dry out and stick to the eggshell. Furthermore, the parents are in a behavioral transition from incubating to feeding, and a major disturbance can prevent that transition from occurring successfully.

GROWTH AND DEVELOPMENT

Birds have developed two main pathways for the development of their young, although there are several gradations. The two main patterns are precocial chicks, which leave the nest soon after hatching, and altricial chicks, which require parental care in the nest for an extended period. Among the secondary cavity nesters, only the ducks are precocial, while the kestrels, owls, and songbirds are altricial.

House Wren eggs and hatchlings.

Precocial Development

Eyes open, able to run and pick up food, precocial ducklings are covered in down at the time of hatching. "Down" does not adequately describe the incredible density of short feathers on a duckling. It looks more like plush and feels as tightly packed as felt. As soon as it is completely dry (which may

Mallard duckling.   LaBelle

take a full day), the down is so light that the ducklings can jump from the nest to the ground with no harm. Probably the webbed feet and minute wings provide some parachute power, too. The down also repels water, so the ducklings can swim for short periods. While still in the nest the ducklings imprint on the female, so they follow her closely, although they feed themselves right from the start.

Altricial Development of Songbirds

Considering the development of altricial songbird nestlings as a series of stages is helpful in estimating the ages of nestlings and in figuring out whether or not a nest was successful. The speed of the progression varies with the species, and also with the weather and food availability. The photos in this series are of Western Bluebirds.

Stage I

The hatchling appears to be not really ready for life outside the egg. It has only a few wisps of long down that do not begin to cover the fragile pink skin. Undeveloped eyes are mere dark bulges under the skin. Yet within hours of breaking out of the egg the neck is strong enough to hold up the head, mouth wide open to beg, and the digestive tract is ready to begin grinding up food brought to the nest by the parents.

Stage II

A few days later, the hatchling already has grown far too large to fold back into the eggshell from which it emerged. Upper and lower eyelids are still sealed together over prominent eyes. At three to five days, the belly and mouth still make up the majority of the nestling. Dark shadows under the skin show where the feathers are beginning to develop. Even though the digestive system of growing birds is amazingly efficient, they do generate waste.

The droppings of birds contain both feces (the dark part) and highly concentrated urine (the white part). Songbird nestlings produce fecal sacs coated in a layer of gel. The parents pick up the droppings and carry them out of the nest without dirtying their bills, and so the nest remains clean while the nestlings are small.

Tree Swallow nest
with Wood Duck
feathers arching
over the eggs.

Tree Swallow
male bringing food
to its nestlings.

Tree Swallow
male carrying
fecal sac out of the
nest.

Stage III

About a week after hatching, the nestling looks like a minia-ture porcupine, covered in quills. The soft tip of each feather is coated with a smooth layer of keratin, the same substance that forms our hair and nails, which helps the feather to push out through the skin as it grows. The eyes are devel-oped by now and the eyelids open, just a slit at first.

Stage IV

As the feathers grow longer, the keratin layer crumbles off in curved, whitish flakes that look like dandruff. The flakes filter down through the nest and accumulate on the floor of the cavity. At eight to twelve days of age, the nestling has enough feather covering to maintain its own body heat. That means that the parents no longer have to spend time brooding the chicks to keep them warm. Good timing, because by now their appetites are ravenous, and no bug is too large to stuff down their welcoming gullets.

Stage V

Fully feathered does not mean capable of flight. It takes several more days or a week for the flight feathers (on the wings and tail) to grow long enough to hold the bird in the air. The muscles and tendons must also be ready. Often you can hear the nestlings flapping their wings inside the nest cavity, which builds up strength for flying. Small wonder that the nest gets packed down flat. The nestlings also vie with each other to receive food brought by the parents. In warm weather and times of plenty, healthy nestlings will compete for the prime position, in the doorway of the nest cavity. The parents can no longer get inside to remove the droppings, which build up in the corners and on the walls of the cavity, and may accumulate over the entire top of the nest.

Altricial Development of Raptors

Nestlings of American Kestrel and owls are already covered with down when they hatch. They take considerably longer to go through the other development stages before fledging.

Oak Titmouse delivering food to its nestlings.

Oak Titmouse nestlings (late Stage III). One is begging for food.

Northern Saw-whet Owl eggs and downy first hatchling.

Violet-green Swallow (Stage V).   LaBelle

FLEDGING

Fledging is the time of first flying. Even though ducklings have been out of the nest for weeks, they have not fledged until their true feathers and muscles have grown enough for flight. Some of the ground nesting songbird chicks leave the nest and scurry around hiding in the vegetation, while young owls may clamber around the branches of the nest tree. Vaux's Swift nestlings make short flights within the large nest chamber for more than a week before they launch on their first true flight. But in general, for the cavity nesting species with altricial development, the timing of leaving the nest is the same as the moment of fledging. The first flight may be short and not very graceful.

Care must be taken to avoid causing nestlings to fledge when they are not yet able to fly well and are much more vulnerable to predation. Many people do not open nest boxes once the nestlings are within a week or so of fledging. Instead, they listen for nestlings in the box or look from a distance to see if parents are still carrying food to it. However, if the lid opens, rather than the front or side of the box, you can open the lid just enough to peer inside without disturbing the young birds into fledging prematurely.

Except for Violet-green Swallows and Vaux's Swifts, most nestlings do not return to the nest cavity. They right away learn to roost in trees or other protected places. They are still fed by the parents for at least a few days. Often the male will continue to feed the fledglings while the female incubates a second (or even a third) clutch of eggs. In bluebirds and several other species, fledglings remain near the nest and assist in feeding the later broods of nestlings. This not only helps the parents and the younger siblings, but also gives the fledglings valuable practice at parenting.

SPECIES AND
NEST SITE PREFERENCES

This chapter concerns the specific natural cavity and nest box placement preferences for each species group, and includes some mammals as well as birds. The next chapter contains suggestions for solving common problems and for orienting and placing boxes to avoid weather-related nest failures, predators, and other difficulties.

When you are evaluating a position to put up a box or create a cavity, try to think like the prospective inhabitants. Look at the approach to that box position, and look from that position out. Ask yourself if the location is likely to meet the needs and preferences of the appropriate species, while avoiding problems from weather and other factors.

What kinds of wildlife will use your nest cavities? Be reasonable in your expectations. First spend some time seeing what species are in the area. Many field guides are available to help you identify species of birds and understand their unique characteristics (see References). For further information on certain species see Organizations and Networking.

House Wren checking possible nest sites.   LaBelle

41

Some of the books and articles on how to build nest boxes also include information on where to place nest boxes for particular species or groups. The California Waterfowl Association (1994), Evans et al. (2002), Henderson (1992), Link (1999), Stokes and Stokes (1990), Varland et al. (1992), and Weston (2001) were used in writing this chapter. Information on natural cavity usage can be found in Brown (1985), Ehrlich et al. (1988), Harrison (1978), and Thomas (1979). The following information uses the snag recommendations from Brown (1985) because larger trees and snags provide better protection, last longer, and are usually preferred, although smaller structures are occasionally used.

CHICKADEES, TITMICE, AND NUTHATCHES

+ Black-capped Chickadee
+ Mountain Chickadee
+ Chestnut-backed Chickadee
- Boreal Chickadee
+ Oak Titmouse
+ Juniper Titmouse
- Red-breasted Nuthatch
+ White-breasted Nuthatch
- Pygmy Nuthatch

+ Frequently uses nest boxes in proper habitat
- Occasionally uses nest boxes in proper habitat

Inhabitants of woodlands and forests, these birds find abundant insects, other arthropods, and seeds in a variety of habitats that include trees. Riparian woods, conifer forests, oak woodlands, orchards, grasslands with some trees, and suburban backyards usually have one or more species from this group. Although nuthatches usually excavate their own holes, and chickadees sometimes do, too, most of the species in this group will readily use nest boxes.

♦   Natural cavities: knotholes, other natural cavities, and small woodpecker holes in live trees or snags at least 23 cm. (9 in.) diameter for chickadees, 38 cm. (15 in.) for titmice, and 43 cm. (17 in.) for nuthatches. Snags: soft snags and pockets of advanced decay in trees or limbs of the same diameters as above for chickadees and nuthatches.

♦ Place boxes on trees of any kind, fence posts, or free-standing poles within 5 m. (about 15 ft.) of trees.

♦ Place each box on a tree with a small branch that curves around to provide a perch about 2 m. (about 6 ft.) out in front of the box, or orient each box toward another tree with a small branch that extends to about 2 m. (about 6 ft.) in front. Avoid a lot of dense branches because nuthatches often prefer a cavity they can enter via a swooping dive from a neighboring tree-top.

♦ Boxes can be as close as 50 m. (about 150 ft.) apart if there is some screening vegetation between them.

♦ Boxes at any height may be used, but ones at least 3 or 4 m. (10 to 12 ft.) above the ground are preferred.

♦ Add 8 to 10 cm. (3 to 4 in.) of wood shavings or small chips in the bottom of the box. Do not use sawdust because it stays wet. The chickadees and nuthatches often carry out chips to form a hollow for the nest. If you fill the box to the lid, or at least to the entrance hole, it will be more similar to a soft snag and attract individuals that prefer to do their own excavating.

Suburban yards provide good habitat for chickadees and nuthatches.

♦ Every two or three years you should move each box, even just a few centimeters up, down, or around the same tree, so that it appears to the birds to be a new nest site. They generally do not use the same cavity for more than a couple of years, which may avoid a build-up of parasitic insects or prevent predators from remembering the site.

WRENS
- Bewick's Wren
+ House Wren

Anywhere there is brush to provide hiding cover and a variety of insects and other arthropods is likely to have wrens of some kind. Brushy draws in rangeland, shrubby backyards, thickets of small trees in forests, dense riparian woods, and overgrown abandoned orchards are some of the more likely places for attracting nesting wrens.

♦ Natural cavities: any type of cavity in any size snag or large limb will do.

♦ Boxes can be placed on trees, fence posts, or buildings where trees or shrubs provide some branchy cover.

♦ No particular orientation is necessary.

♦ Space boxes 30 m. (about 100 ft.) apart or more, with screening vegetation or a structure in between.

♦ Boxes at any height may be used, but ones at least 1½ to 3 m. (5 to 10 ft.) above ground are preferred.

Wrens prosper in brushy habitat with dense, branchy trees.

BLUEBIRDS AND FLYCATCHERS

+ Ash-throated Flycatcher
+ Western Bluebird
+ Mountain Bluebird

Birds of open country with scattered trees, these species can be attracted to boxes in many settings. Open oak woods, grassland with junipers (or sometimes just with fence posts), open conifer stands, forest edges, logged or burned areas with residual trees, orchards, farms, vineyards, and some suburban areas are all good possibilities. Bluebirds prosper where they can perch or hover to see insects moving in sparse or very short vegetation. Flycatchers forage around individual trees or small groups. Be happy if you get even one flycatcher nest, and be patient because more will probably come within a few years.

- Natural cavities: knotholes, other natural cavities, and medium to large woodpecker holes in live trees or snags at least 38 cm. (15 in.) diameter.

- Place boxes on freestanding poles, fence posts, or tree trunks. If on trees, choose ones with few or no lower branches, or remove all branches from a wide area around where the box will be.

- Orient the box to avoid spring storm winds, and to face good foraging habitat. If possible, orient the box towards a tree, tall shrub, or fence that is 15 to 50 m. (about 50-150 ft.) away. On their first flight from

Bluebirds and flycatchers prefer open areas with scattered trees.   LaBelle the box the young birds should not have to land on the ground where they and their parents may be more vulnerable to predators.

♦ Unless you are putting up only two or three boxes, space them at least 100 m. (about 350 ft.) apart, preferably more.

♦ Boxes do not need to be placed any higher than 1½ m. (5 ft.) above the ground, except where cats or snakes might be a problem.

SWALLOWS

+ Purple Martin
+ Tree Swallow
+ Violet-green Swallow

Enjoyed for their swooping flight while foraging for high flying insects, swallows require a lot more space than their small size and marvelous agility would indicate. Generally, they prefer to be near large ponds, marshes, or rivers that provide abundant small insects as well as duck feathers for nests. If there is water within a kilometer (about ½ mile), meadows, pastures, rangeland, farms, and suburban yards can provide good habitat for swallows.

♦ Natural cavities: knotholes, other natural cavities, and any size woodpecker holes in live trees or snags at

A pair of Purple Martins, largest of the swallows.   LaBelle

least 38 cm. (15 in.) diameter for small swallows, and medium to large woodpecker or other holes in the same size live trees or snags for Purple Martin.

♦ Boxes on free-standing poles most readily attract swallows; however, boxes can be placed on fence posts, tall trees, or buildings. Make sure there are no branches or other trees anywhere near the boxes.

♦ Purple Martins nest in small colonies, so place at least three boxes within 10 m. (about 30 ft.) of each other. However, the subspecies in this region does not use the huge martin apartment houses common in the eastern United States. In this region, the best setup is a very tall pole with cross-arms holding six or eight hanging gourds. Martins may need a source of mud for the sill they often build on the front of the nest.

Students putting up nest boxes for swallows.   LaBelle

Gourds for Purple Martins can be lowered for checking and cleaning.

♦ Orient boxes away from spring storms and towards the most open water or low vegetation area.

♦ For any of the swallows, boxes can be as close as 10 m. (about 30 ft.) apart. Placing them farther apart and facing them in slightly different directions may avoid some of the fighting over what is a scarce resource in a natural setting.

♦ Swallows will use boxes placed as low as 1½ m. (5 ft.) but are more likely to use ones that are 3 or 4 m. (10 to 12 ft.) above ground. Boxes or gourds for martins should be as high as safety allows.

WATERFOWL

+ Wood Duck
- Common Goldeneye
- Barrow's Goldeneye
- Bufflehead
+ Hooded Merganser
- Common Merganser

Obviously, nest boxes for cavity nesting ducks need to be near water. Ponds, swamps, sloughs, or quiet backwaters of rivers can provide good habitat if they have aquatic vegetation, emergent or shoreline plants with edible seeds, and plenty of invertebrates. Nest platforms and other structures have been developed for geese and other water birds, but these are beyond the scope of this book.

♦ Natural cavities: knotholes, other natural cavities, and large woodpecker holes in live trees or snags at least 64 cm. (25 in.) diameter, and medium woodpecker holes in trees and snags at least 43 cm. (17 in.) for Bufflehead and Hooded Merganser.

♦ Boxes can be placed on free-standing posts in water, if the water level does not fluctuate too much. For a new area, another good position is on trees at the water's edge, especially those that lean slightly out over the water. But once ducks know about the boxes, they may be more apt to use ones placed back in the trees up to 75 m. (250 ft.) away from the water, probably because these are less visible to potential predators.

♦ Ducklings can walk quite a distance to water, but there must be an easy route for them, so avoid obstacles such as huge logs and blackberry tangles. Thorny shrubs or vines do not make a good landing site for the ducklings' jump down from the nest box, either.

♦ Boxes should face the water or an opening between trees. Make sure that the approach to the entrance hole is easy for the female. She barely slows down, so avoid or remove any branches growing in front of the box, and plan on annual pruning if necessary to keep the approach open.

♦ Either space the boxes at least 100 m. (about 350 ft.) apart, position them with screening vegetation in between, or face them away from each other. Otherwise, several females may lay eggs in the same nest. This can produce more ducklings, but more often all of the eggs are abandoned.

♦ Boxes can be placed only 1½ m. (5 ft.) above water if they are on poles. If placed on trees on the shore, they are less noticeable to predators if placed at least 4 m. (15 ft.) above ground.

Boxes facing water or an opening are apt to attract ducks.   LaBelle

♦ Add 10 to 15 cm. (4 to 6 in.) of wood shavings or small chips, but not sawdust, in the bottom of the box.

OWLS AND KESTRELS

+ American Kestrel
+ Barn Owl
- Flammulated Owl
+ Western Screech-Owl
- Northern Hawk Owl
- Northern Pygmy-Owl
- Boreal Owl
+ Northern Saw-whet Owl

Most of the cavity nesting owls are forest or woodland dwellers, but the Barn Owl and American Kestrel prefer open country. Most of these raptors will nest along forest edges, riparian areas, and in any habitats with scattered trees, such as orchards, oak woodlands, or juniper savannahs. Northern Pygmy-Owl and Boreal Owl prefer more dense forest habitat. It will require considerable knowledge of habitat preferences, as well as patience and quite a few boxes, to entice most of the little owl species to use nest boxes.

♦ Natural cavities: knotholes, other natural cavities, and medium to large woodpecker holes in live trees or snags at least 43 cm. (17 in.) diameter, and large holes in trees and snags at least 64 cm. (25 in.) diameter for Barn Owl.

♦ Place nest boxes on large trees or poles. Boxes for Barn Owls or kestrels can be placed inside an open barn. Boxes for kestrels are probably best placed in a different area from small boxes for songbirds; otherwise, kestrel parents may learn to snatch songbird nestlings to feed their own youngsters.

♦ Generally, the orientation of the boxes is not a key consideration, except to avoid prevailing storms.

♦ Raptors require large foraging territories. For kestrels, 800 m. (1/2 mile) apart may be necessary if the boxes get much use. For owls, space boxes at least 100 m.

Student checking a box for owls.   Kestrels prefer very open areas.

(about 300 ft.) apart. On the other hand, few boxes will be used by owls, so it is probably good to provide several choices.

♦ Boxes should be placed at a minimum height of 4 m. (about 12 ft.) or as high as safety allows. Remember safety in planning for maintenance as well as initial placement.

♦ Add 10 to 15 cm. (4 to 6 in.) of wood shavings or chips, but not sawdust, in the bottom of the box.

♦ In forest habitats, boxes may need to be moved every few years to prevent predators learning the locations. Boreal Owls, and possibly others, may only use a particular box once, perhaps because of the increasing likelihood of predation.

WOODPECKERS

Woodpeckers usually excavate their own nest chambers and have specific snag preferences (Brown 1985, Lundquist and Mariani 1991, Thomas 1979). However, if snags are not available Northern Flickers and other woodpeckers will sometimes use nest boxes. It is important to understand, however, that snags also provide the beetle grubs, ants, and other insects that are often the sole food for woodpeckers. Even if you don't have great foraging habitat, if a flicker persists in drilling a hole in the siding of your house, try putting up a nest box. You might even need to cover its hole with the box, but make sure you do not trap anyone inside the hole. Pack the box full to the lid or at least to the entrance hole with wood shavings or chips, so the woodpecker can do the excavating. If the flicker or other woodpecker is just drumming on your house, often on a metal vent cover, you also might try building a good metal drum somewhere in your yard where it is less apt to drive you crazy.

Northern Flicker female feeding its nestlings in a snag.   LaBelle

OTHER BIRDS

Researchers working with several other birds have developed nest boxes for studying and assisting these species. Boxes buried in soil have been successfully used by both Burrowing Owl (Henderson 1992, Marshall et al. 2003) and Rhinoceros Auklet (Sydeman 2002). Boxes that are 3 ½ m. (12 ft.) above ground and attached to trees have proven successful for Vaux's Swift (Bull 2002). Small lean-to boxes have been used by Brown Creepers (Strycker 2003).

While most of us will not have the opportunity to try boxes for Burrowing Owls or Rhinoceros Auklets, we can put up a swift box in many settings, including towns and suburban neighborhoods. However, it is a *major* undertaking. In the eastern United States, false chimneys are constructed just for the Chimney Swifts there (see Driftwood Wildlife Association in Organizations and Networking, page 135). Please allow Vaux's Swifts to use your chimney if the inside is rough brick or concrete. The one little nest will not make much mess. However, if larger numbers roost in the chimney in the fall (which seems to occur after a successful nest there), you may need to clean droppings out by opening the damper

Vaux's Swift nest was glued with saliva into a corner of a chimney.   LaBelle

after the swifts have left. If your furnace has a separate vent, cap it or cover it with wire mesh, but leave the main chimney cap off in summer and don't use the fireplace until the swifts migrate south, usually in early October.

A far easier endeavor than building a swift box or cleaning the chimney is to build very simple lean-tos for Brown Creepers, which usually nest under a section of bark that has partially separated from a tree trunk (see page 79). Further information on providing cavities and where to place boxes for each of these species can be found in the chapter on Additional Sources of Information.

Northern Flying Squirrel looking out of a nest box built for ducks.
LaBelle

SQUIRRELS

Even though this book is about birds, it is important for nest box monitors to realize that some native mammals need our help, too. The Douglas Squirrel, Western Grey Squirrel, and probably all of the chipmunk species in the region can be nuisances at bird feeders and definitely prey on bird eggs and nestlings. However, birds and mammals alike are suffering from loss of habitat and the invasion of domestic cats and exotic wildlife. The Northern Flying Squirrel has also lost out where woods and forests have been cut down and natural cavities are scarce. Several Northern Flying Squirrels will use a duck or owl box for hibernation, and an individual female will use a small box for raising her young. In fact, putting up nest boxes just for flying squirrels may increase

Douglas Squirrels often use nest boxes in wooded areas.

their populations and therefore enhance a food source for Northern Spotted Owls in marginal or young forest habitat (PNW Forestry Sciences Lab 1993). All these native mammals should be welcomed and encouraged in places where they will not cause trouble in your bird nest boxes.

Please do be careful when monitoring boxes, because any rodents could carry Hanta virus, which could infect you if dust from dried droppings and urine gets in your eyes, nose, or mouth (see page 90).

BATS

Monitoring bats is beyond the scope of this manual because it requires different methods, not to mention specialized equipment and training just to identify the bat species. But these invaluable and beautiful little mammals need all the help we can give them, so please put up some boxes designed for them, too. Information is available in Tuttle and Hensley (2001), Link (1999), and the Bat Conservation International website (see page 135). Forest edges and openings, farmlands and orchards, and suburban neighborhoods with well established trees all have potential for bat house occupation, as do sites near marshes, ponds, and open streams. Many bats live in caves and rock crevices, but in this region several species use large trees, raising young and roosting inside hollow trunks or in crevices and under the edges of thick bark. Wooden bat boxes can provide similar shelters.

Sunny and wind-sheltered places are favored by bats. Make sure there are no branches or other obstructions near the box, particularly under it. You may need to paint or stain the boxes a dark color to absorb even more of the sun's heat. Dillingham and co-authors (2003) found that boxes facing south or east, and facing open areas, were used most often by forest-dwelling bats. Even though the prevailing storm winds come from the southwest in much of this region, gaining sun warmth, especially in the morning, seems to be the most important factor. Boxes should be placed at least 4 m. (about 12 ft.) above ground or as high as is safely possible. You will not need to reach the box every time you check it. Just look up into it with a flashlight, and look for droppings underneath.

Boxes for bats should be in sunny locations, with no obstructing branches under the opening which is at the bottom.

PROBLEMS AND SOLUTIONS

If you are just starting a nest box program and things are not going the way you planned, do not lose heart. Unwanted nest box occupants, no occupants, dead occupants. We have all experienced problems with our boxes, and many inventive and dedicated people have worked out various solutions. In particular, the North American Bluebird Society and the Bluebird Recovery Program have studied alternative ways of dealing with assorted difficulties in boxes for songbirds (see Organizations and Networking, and References). The following are the most commonly encountered problems, with one or more ways to correct them.

WEATHER

We cannot change the weather, but we can sometimes alleviate its harshest effects on birds. In the Pacific Northwest, May is often the unkindest month of the year. Just when most bird species are in the midst of nesting, the weather often turns cold and buckets of rain fall. Insects die or go into hiding. If bad weather persists, many bird parents must abandon their eggs or nestlings. At the other extreme, sudden very hot weather can also stress birds, and even normal summer weather can cause problems for second nests, individual bird pairs that start nesting late, and late-breeding species.

Nest box design – Our best efforts at designing nest boxes can never match the efficiency of a woodpecker cavity. However, we can modify basic designs to come a little closer in areas where breeding season weather causes frequent nest failures. If hot or cold temperatures are the issue, build your nest boxes out of thicker wood to provide better insulation. In hot areas, add more ventilation holes. In cold areas, reduce the number. Where it is cold early and hot late in the breeding season, have lots of ventilation but stuff felt insulation in the holes until the weather warms up. If rain might be a problem, build the box with a large lid that overhangs several inches on the front and sides. Make sure the lid fits tightly on the rim of the box all the way around and does not allow water to trickle in. If necessary, add a piece of plastic over the lid to direct the water elsewhere.

Nest box position and orientation – The best direction to orient nest boxes is a subject of much discussion among box monitors. However, avoiding the prevailing direction of spring storms should probably be your primary consideration. In this region, wind accompanying storms usually comes from the southwest, so nests may do best in boxes oriented northeast. Some people place boxes on the underside of slightly tilting trees or posts, so that rain is less likely to enter the boxes. The northeast side of trees or posts also allows the greatest heat gain in the morning from sun striking the side of the box, while also providing shade from the hottest afternoon sun (Navratil 2002). Lower boxes may be warmed by heat radiating up from the ground, while higher boxes may be cooled by catching additional breezes.

Water – In areas where hot weather causes stress to nesting birds, providing a water source can be a life saver. In

Many nests are successful in boxes oriented to catch morning sun.

extreme heat, parent birds will soak their belly feathers with water and mud, which they carry back into the nest to cool the chicks. A birdbath in your yard is a wonderful addition. If you have enough property for a pond, make sure you design it with some very shallow, muddy edges, and logs or large branches angling down into the water, so that birds can easily walk into the water.

Feeding – Some nest box monitors raise mealworms, which they regularly place in special bird feeders near active nests (see bluebird groups in Organizations and Networking). In a prolonged period of bad weather, a steady source of mealworms can help parent birds keep nestlings alive. This may demand daily replenishing in the feeder. Other monitors argue that artificial feeding interferes with natural selection and makes birds dependent on humans and therefore not truly wild. Providing diverse, high-quality habitat that produces natural foods is certainly the best long-term assistance we can give to wildlife.

EMPTY BOXES

You have built and put up the most beautiful boxes in the world, but nobody uses them. What to do?

Be patient. If there have never been nest boxes in your area before, the birds may see them as dangerous traps rather than homes. After a year of weathering (several years for duck boxes), the birds will become familiar with them in the landscape and begin to investigate.

Try different locations. Placing a nest box right beside the front window may be great for you to watch, but there may be too much activity for birds to feel safe. See what species actually occur on the site. Then match your box locations to the needs and preferences of those species (see the previous chapter). Also read through the other problems in this section to make sure you do not trade one difficulty for another by choosing a different problem location.

UNWANTED OCCUPANTS

This is one of the most ornery issues for nest box monitors to confront. Remember your original objectives for putting up boxes before you tackle invaders. If you are trying to help native wildlife, can you be objective and learn to welcome other natives besides your favorite species? Most importantly, though, if the only occupants of your boxes are the alien invaders (European Starlings and House Sparrows), think about whether or not you should even have nest boxes on the site.

Your less favorite native birds – If you really just want one species out of all the wonderful natives that might use your nest boxes, then you will have to pay close attention to the precise location preferences of the different birds in your area (see the previous chapter). Remember that all native birds are protected species. It is unlawful to destroy an active nest or remove eggs or chicks of even the most aggressive native House Wren or Violet-green Swallow. Every one

In nature, birds must fight for scarce nest cavities. Left: Violet-green Swallow male feeding nestling. Right: male Tree Swallow guarding nest box.

House Wren, a native species, brings food to its mate who feeds it to the hatchlings while brooding them to keep them warm.   LaBelle

of the native cavity nesting species needs our help, so please put up enough boxes to welcome them all. If you notice extreme levels of competition over one or several boxes, consider putting up additional boxes. Spread them farther apart and orient them so that they do not face each other, or place boxes in pairs 0 to 8 m. (25 ft.) apart, with the pairs placed at least 100 m. (300 ft.) apart (Brown 2002).

House Sparrow (English Sparrow) – A cute little bird in its native British Isles, it does *not* belong here. Moreover, it is the most aggressive species in the region for taking over nesting cavities from the native birds. Known to puncture eggs, kill nestlings, and even occasionally kill incubating females, it is a serious factor in the decline of native bird populations. It *must not* be permitted to raise its own chicks in your nest boxes. If you are not willing to deal with House Sparrows (even humanely kill them, if necessary), then you should *not* put up nest boxes where they occur!

◆   Avoid House Sparrow habitat – Put boxes up far away from barns or other structures where grain is apt to be spilled. Do not put boxes up near homes where people allow House Sparrows to use bird feeders. Do not put birdseed containing millet in your feeders, and encourage neighbors not to. Look and listen for House Sparrows in your area before putting up nest boxes.

♦ Exclude House Sparrows from boxes – If your boxes are designed for the smallest birds, the chickadees, wrens, and nuthatches, make sure the hole diameter is the recommended size (see page 84). Then the hole will be barely large enough for these natives and too tight for the House Sparrow. Nest boxes with a horizontal slot opening or a diamond-shaped hole rather than a round hole will permit native swallows to enter, because of their low and broad-shouldered shape,

while excluding the taller, larger-headed House Sparrows. Davis and Roca (1995) found that a $1^{1}/_{8}$ in. tall slot opening excluded House Sparrows and was actually preferred by bluebirds. A dried and cleaned out gourd with an entrance hole, hung where the gourd will sway, may deter House Sparrows while being readily accepted by Purple Martins and other native swallows. For more information, contact the Purple Martin Conservation Association (see page 135).

A non-native House Sparrow female at a nest box.   LaBelle

♦   Close nest boxes for the winter – Since House Sparrows are residents and do not migrate for the winter, they will start nesting long before the migrants return in the spring. If you have just a couple of boxes, take them down each year (or block the entrance holes) right after the breeding season and do not put them back up until the native species are definitely ready to nest the next spring. You may be able to avoid House Sparrow problems by managing your boxes just for late nesting species like swallows and House Wrens (see pages 44 and 46).

♦ Destroy House Sparrows and their nests – If you see House Sparrows entering your nest box, either take it down or prepare for battle. Since House Sparrows are not native, it is legal to destroy them and their nests, and you do not need any permit. Remove the nest, and continue removing nests every few days. If there are eggs, please remove and break them. As nasty as that sounds, it is easier than killing House Sparrow nestlings (by putting them in a plastic bag in the freezer). And it is far better than allowing House Sparrows to raise their young, thereby contributing to the decline of native bird species. The only way to finally win the battle is to remove the adults. The easiest way is to catch them in a live trap. Bait it with fluffy feathers or other nest material when they are building a nest, or use seeds for bait. *Do not* just take the adult House Sparrows away and release them elsewhere, because they will easily return or cause problems somewhere else. If you cannot humanely kill them yourself (by shooting them or breaking their necks), find a falconer or wildlife rehabilitation center that will accept live House Sparrows to feed to hawks.

European Starling – This vocal clown of the bird world does not belong here either. Not as violent as the House Sparrow, it is just as clever and adaptable, even patiently waiting for a flicker to finish excavating a cavity before bullying it away. The starling has been implicated in declining populations of several native species, while its own flocks reach a stunning magnitude. Please be ruthless in discouraging this species, too.

♦ Avoid starling habitat – Make sure that your nest boxes are not placed near barns or in other locations where spilled grain or other feed is likely. Do not put boxes up near homes where people allow starlings to use bird feeders. Look and listen for this species in your area before putting up nest boxes.

♦ Exclude starlings from nest boxes – Starlings generally are easy to exclude from nest boxes designed for songbirds because they are slightly bulkier than even the Mountain Bluebird and Ash-throated Flycatcher. Using the smallest recommended hole diameter for the native songbird species usually will prevent starlings from using the box (see page 84). Be alert to hole enlargement by flickers and rodents, and replace the box or add a new front with the proper hole size. Using a slot entrance will allow low and broad-shouldered Purple Martins to enter while preventing use by the taller starlings. Prepared gourds hung for Purple Martins are not often used by starlings.

A slot opening excludes non-native species, and allows several Tree Swallow nestlings to beg at the same time.   LaBelle

♦ Destroy starlings and their nests – If starlings nest in boxes with a large entrance hole, such as those for ducks or owls, please treat them as severely, albeit humanely, as House Sparrows (see above).

Rodents – Chipmunks, squirrels, and mice often enjoy nest boxes put up for birds. Many of these pesky critters are native species, too, and valuable parts of the ecosystem. If you have quite a few boxes up and only a couple are used by native rodents each year, try to be charitable and accept them.

However, if you are getting non-native Fox Squirrels in your area, you need to take action. The Fox Squirrel, introduced from the East Coast and the Midwest, is much larger than the natives. It can reach down farther into nest boxes to raid bird nests, and it can outcompete the native squirrels for food and nesting cavities. If your boxes are attracting Fox Squirrels, or native rodents more often than birds, and you are worried about Hanta virus – as you should be – here are some suggestions. Also see those under "Predation" below.

♦ Avoid rodent habitat – Since rodents are so adaptable, this can be difficult. Place nest boxes in the most open locations and positions available that will still attract the native birds appropriate to the site. In particular, avoid or clear away brush and branches at the base of the tree used for plac-

A Fox Squirrel (non-native) took over a nest box built for owls.   LaBelle

A native Northern Flying Squirrel defends her nest, with her ears folded back to protect them .

A Northern Flying Squirrel newborn already has a wrinkled fold of loose skin along each side.

Chipmunks are native squirrel species that often use nest boxes.

ing each box. A single tree trunk is less attractive to rodents than a divided tree or a cluster of trunks. Rodents often hide in or under rock-jacks used in fences, so, unless the fence post is extra tall and the box far above the rock-jack, this is usually a location to avoid. Of course, if a rattlesnake lives there the birds can safely use the box, but you would have to use extra caution checking it. A gate post or fence "H" may also be a problem if the box is placed just above an angled strut or brace that provides an easy ramp for rodents going to and from the box.

◆ Close nest boxes for the fall and winter – Many rodents build nests in boxes during the fall and may hibernate or base their winter operations in them. Wintering rodents generally leave a large accumulation of droppings in one corner, the most serious Hanta virus threat. Remove the boxes right after the bird nesting season, or if that is not practical plug the entrance holes or leave the lids off. Make sure to replace or reopen them in late winter if you want to attract resident native birds such as chickadees.

◆ Remove rodent nests – As soon as you notice definite signs of rodent use, remove the nest and temporarily leave the lid off to discourage them. However, if the first thing you notice is

Squirrel nest of leaves and trash.
LaBelle

a nest full of babies, just enjoy the cute little things and let them be, *if* they are a native species. They will leave a scrupulously clean nest (the mother eats the droppings the way cats and dogs do), very different from the winter nest. Remove the nest after the family has left. Non-native Fox Squirrels should be live-trapped and humanely killed or taken to a wildlife rehabilitation center.

♦ Repel rodents – Because mammals are more reliant on their sense of smell than birds, it may be possible to prevent rodents from taking over a box by using a scent that repels them. Make sure that the scent you try is not a source of volatile chemicals harmful to them, to birds, or to you. Strong herbs? Perfumes? Cat urine? How desperate are you?

PREDATION

Many nest box programs are lucky and suffer few losses to predation. While infrequent losses to native predators are just part of the natural world (kestrels have to feed their youngsters, too), persistent predation losses require attention. Before panicking, however, make sure that the problem really is predators killing eggs or nestlings, rather than scavengers eating them after they died during a period of cold, wet weather. Starting with the proper design and placement of nest boxes is the best way to prevent predation, and is far easier than correcting a problem after the predators have gotten used to associating nest boxes with food. Placing nest boxes high up on branch-free tree trunks can stymie many predators, but carrying a ladder to monitor boxes is also a nuisance. In some areas, it may be necessary to mount all of your nest boxes on free-standing, smooth, round poles (PVC electrical conduit or metal pipe), and you may need to add predator guards as described in the North American Bluebird Society website and publications (see page 135).

House Sparrow and European Starling are discussed in previous sections, because when they kill other birds it is not really an act of predation. It is the nest cavity that they want.

Rodents are also discussed in the previous section. But sometimes rodents raid nests to eat eggs or small nestlings. Non-native Fox Squirrels are a worse problem than the native Douglas and Red Squirrels (Chickarees). Being larger, they can reach farther down into a box to pull out the chicks, although all squirrels can simply chew their way into a box. Wrapping the box in sheet metal or just putting a piece with the correct size hole over the front may stop the chewing, but may be hard on the birds' feet. Smearing a paste of cayenne pepper or curry powder in bands around the tree both above and below the box may work as an emergency treatment. Better long-term solutions are mounting boxes on smooth poles or putting a cone-shaped baffle or a wide band of sheet metal around the post or tree below the box. If squirrels can jump to the box from the branches of neighboring trees, also put a baffle above the box.

Raccoon and opossum – Although the Raccoon is a native species, its populations have grown to unnatural densities in every area where humans live in this region, and it has severely impacted certain bird species. Introduced to this region, the Virginia Opossum quickly became numerous and widespread. In some areas, Raccoons have apparently outcompeted them so their numbers have dropped again. Many people purposely feed Raccoons, not realizing they are raising potentially dangerous dependents as well as upsetting natural predator-prey relationships. Just as bad, people inadvertently feed both Raccoons and opossums by

Owl nest box protected from predators by sheet metal bands. LaBelle

leaving food outside for their dogs and cats. Bird feeders are often placed where these mammals can get to them. Human garbage has also become food for these species in places where people camp out. *Not* providing food for Raccoons and opossums, and educating others about the problem, are the most effective ways you can help prevent their predation of nests. Immediate problems can be addressed by the sheet metal guards described above. Other solutions are to add a longer entryway into the box using wire mesh or ready-made predator guards, or to put some scent repellant on or next to the box. Smooth poles or baffles are the only long-term solutions if Raccoons or opossums are a major problem in your area.

Cats – Is your cat an indoor cat or one that can kill native birds? Feral cats are certainly a problem, but well fed pets with good homes and loving owners also wreak havoc among birds and other small wildlife. If you think a cat would be unhappy and a nuisance living in your home, please do not own a cat. If feral cats and neighbors' pets learn to raid nest boxes, the short-term solutions are the smooth poles or baffles described above. Long-term solutions are education and getting rid of feral cats by live-trapping and taking them to a pet shelter.

Gopher Snakes are usually very gentle and they eat many rodents.

Snakes – Gopher snakes (bullsnakes) are adept at climbing trees, and can enter nest boxes to eat eggs and nestlings, although they are more apt to eat rodents. Rattlesnakes are too heavy-bodied to climb trees, much less enter boxes, but other species could occasionally raid a nest. In most places the problem is quite rare. If snake predation does become a problem in your nest boxes, metal baffles around the post or tree under the boxes may solve it. Please remember that these snakes are protected native species, fascinating and beautiful, and their importance in the ecosystems should be respected.

Predatory birds – Kestrels, other small hawks, and most of the Corvids (certainly Steller's Jay, Scrub Jay, American Crow, and Common Raven) are capable of pulling nestlings out of boxes. They are most apt to snatch an older nestling that sticks its head out the hole to accept food from its parents. They also have been seen poking their heads into nest box entrance holes. This is a learned behavior that can re-

sult in individual predatory birds making the rounds of boxes, causing many losses of nestlings, and teaching other individuals to do the same. There are several ways to prevent predatory birds from finding easy pickings in your nest boxes:

1. Never put up a shallow box, less than 15 cm. (6 in.) from the hole to the bottom of the box.
2. Clean out used nests at least annually so they do not fill the lower part of the box.
3. Replace the front of boxes that have a hole larger than recommended.

American Kestrel female has just fed a grasshopper to her nestlings.   LaBelle

4. Never put up a box with a perch or ledge under the hole.
5. Never put up a box where a predator can use a fence wire, adjacent branch, or other perch for easy access.
6. Try lids with a wider overhang to the front and sides.
7. Wire mesh predator guards on the entrance hole also work well.

Predatory birds, too, are protected native species and a valuable part of their wildlife communities.

Other predators – Now and then an American Black Bear discovers nest boxes. Generally, it has previously discovered bird feeders, the open tray type that invite all comers and spread quantities of seed on the ground. The only reasonable response is to stop feeding birds and to take down nest boxes for a full year until the bear has moved to greener pastures and established other feeding patterns. After a year, closed feeders and nest boxes may be safe. Very rarely a box check will reveal a satisfied weasel where a bunch of nestlings were anticipated. Probably the best response is just to be thrilled to observe another facet of the natural world and a wild animal most people never get to see. In forested areas, Pine Marten prey on nesting owls, and may learn where to return for an annual luncheon. Moving nest boxes every few years may reduce predation and increase owl usage of boxes, as Heather Bateman (2001) found while studying Boreal Owls in Colorado.

INSECTS AND OTHER ARTHROPODS

In most cases insects, spiders, and the like that are found in a box are not a problem, but they may be an indication of a problem. Flies buzzing around a box or ants crawling over it usually mean that there are dead nestlings or cracked eggs, often covered by a new nest. With any insects or other arthropods, please do not use pesticides, because of their unintended effects, including the killing of non-target organisms.

Sowbugs (Pillbugs) and Earwigs – Finding these under nest material indicates that rain can get into the box. Move

Hornets and Yellowjackets use nest boxes for small early nests and multi-tiered nests that are fiercely defended in late summer.

or redesign the box (see page 57). Earwigs are misunderstood beneficial predators of harmful garden insects. However, sowbugs can carry parasites lethal to birds, which usually only eat them in cold, wet springs when other food sources are scarce, according to Elsie Eltzroth (2000), Western Bluebird expert from Oregon.

Wasps and Bees – Various types of wasps occasionally take over an inactive box. If they are yellowjackets or hornets, you just have to abandon that box for the year to avoid being stung. Paper wasps are much less apt to sting. They often move in for the winter, usually just one or a few per box. On a cold fall day they are very slow and can safely be brushed out of the box. But you should feel honored if a bumblebee moves into an abandoned nest in a box, because there are several native species that are declining and need our help. Please let bumblebees raise their young before cleaning out the box.

Blowflies – Blowflies lay their eggs in nest material. The larvae or grubs crawl up to the nestlings and suck blood from them. If the nestlings are growing fast, blowfly infestations are not a problem. When food is scarce (usually when the weather is cool and damp), blowflies may contribute to nestling deaths. If you notice the fat gray grubs attached to the nestlings, you can pull them off, except if your box is part of a research project. Damp nests, especially ones with visible grubs, can be replaced with dry grasses (see page 93). The reddish-brown blowfly pupae underneath a nest can be removed, too. On the other hand, Washington entomologist Terry Whitworth (2000) advises that parasites naturally cull out nestlings that are less apt to survive anyway.

VANDALISM

Occasional pranks that do not harm nesting birds can be tolerated. However, if people frequently use nest boxes for target shooting, throw rocks at boxes, or steal either the boxes or eggs inside them, you have a problem. Attractively painted boxes may be particularly vulnerable to theft, as are the gourds used for Purple Martin, according to Washington expert Kevin Li (personal communication, 2003). Education is probably the only long-term solution for most vandalism. Signs on the boxes might work, but better yet is to enlist the neighborhood kids to help monitor your boxes. Contact the local school and give programs about birds and what you are trying to do to help them. If adults are causing the problem, their kids may educate them.

MISCELLANEOUS

Strange things can happen to nest boxes while your back is turned. Look for clues, then use common sense and inventiveness. For instance, you discover a nest box off the tree or fence post, lying on the ground. Aha, there is some fur on the outside bottom corner, left when a horse used the box to scratch an itch or a cow bumped it in passing. Place the box higher, or on a tree with a couple of jutting branches well below the box, or on the other side of the post from a busy path. Another solution is to place a couple of rocks or cut branches on the ground under the box to divert traffic and discourage loitering under the box.

MAKING HOMES FOR WILDLIFE

Consider the trade-offs. You build nest boxes to help chickadees and bluebirds. But what if the wood you use comes from a tree that provided habitat for a Spotted Owl? Stan Kostka, Purple Martin expert from Washington, worries that putting up nest boxes in too many places where natural cavities are still available may lead to populations of birds that are unnecessarily dependent on humans for nesting habitat (personal communication, 2003). Matthew Evans and co-authors (2002) are concerned that putting up many nest boxes may increase populations of particular cavity nesting birds at the expense of other species in that wildlife community.

Even if you use recycled construction lumber or scrap wood, building nest boxes is not the best or only way to provide homes for secondary cavity nesting species. Snags that are maintained or created provide not only housing but also foraging areas for wildlife, as well as fulfilling other ecosystem functions. Think outside the box. You can be as opportunistic and inventive as the birds.

CREATING SNAGS

Of course, the first thing to attempt is just leaving a dead or partially decayed tree stand-

Maple snag in front yard.   LaBelle

ing. Put guy wires on it if you are worried about it falling on your house, or on people and playground equipment at your local park. Or have a professional tree expert take some of the top off so the snag is not tall enough to reach a structure if it does fall. It is very satisfying to maintain a snag, and to watch Downy Woodpeckers excavate a nest hole one year and chickadees move into it the following year. Try it on your property, or work with your parks bureau to try to keep a few snags at a neighborhood park. Talk to the school district about saving snags on school grounds.

If a live tree must be removed, what about turning it into a snag? A professional can top the tree or girdle the trunk, preferably up high, just below the branches. If the tree does not die right away, it may be necessary to place strips of copper wire or other copper in the girdled groove, right against the still live cambium layer. If you are removing the tree because it was too close to a building, consider moving a long section of it and erecting it in a safer spot, with the base set in concrete in the ground. If you are not convinced your neighbors will appreciate the beauty of your backyard snag, leave a couple of low branch stubs or attach metal brackets and hang some flower baskets. The hummingbirds will love them. Native flowers are best. Try yellow monkeyflower, bleeding heart, twinflower, or penstemons. If those are not available, use domesticated nasturtiums or fuchsia.

Black-capped Chickadees often make their nests in old Downy Woodpecker cavities.   LaBelle

Snag habitat can be created and maintained on a much

larger scale, too (Brown 2000, Bull et al. 1997, Hildebrand and Parks 2002, Huss et al. 2002, PNW Forestry Sciences Lab 1993). In a forested setting, including timber sales that will leave some trees for wildlife, certain trees can be killed specifically to provide snags. This is usually accomplished by a professional climber who can either cut the top out, place explosives to blast the top out, or girdle the tree under the canopy branches. The top or trunk of a live tree or created snag can be inoculated with disease organisms that will initiate the rotting process there, rather than at the base, which would cause the snag to fall sooner. There are specialists with extensive experience in these skills, for instance, Frontier Tree and Wildlife (see page 135).

According to Evelyn Bull and co-authors (1997) and Lundquist and Mariani (1991), the features of snags and partially decayed trees used by most cavity nesting wildlife include the following:

♦ large diameter trunk

♦ pockets of soft, decayed wood

♦ old woodpecker holes or natural cavities from wounds (e.g., knotholes where branches broke off)

♦ bark that is thick, flaking, or loosening

♦ crevices, deep furrows, and other irregularities in the bark or outer wood

♦ hollow trunk or top.

Live tree with the top blasted out, which will eventually become a snag.   LaBelle

Even though close monitoring of nests in snags is more difficult than in boxes, and impossible in tall and unstable snags, much good information can be gathered with binoculars or a mirror and light mounted on a pole.

CREATING CAVITIES

If you tried any of the snag creation methods described previously but the woodpeckers failed to create cavities, try creating them yourself, or find a chainsaw specialist to help you out. Practice on a log, or experiment with one or two trees on a large property or woodlot, if that is an option.

A chainsaw can be used to hollow out a small section of a live tree or a hard snag (PNW Forestry Sciences Lab. 1993, Scott 1987). You may be able to use hand tools on a soft snag. Carve out the cavity and make a new front with an entrance hole. The new front can be made from scrap wood or, for a more natural appearance, by cutting an outer slab off of a section of log or firewood. In a new snag with wood that is still hard, you can also open up a larger cavity through what will be the back. Make an entrance hole from your opened section through what will be the front. Then cover the back

Making a notch for bats or Brown Creepers.   LaBelle

Making a lean-to house for Brown Creepers.   LaBelle

opening with a thick piece of scrap wood, removable for cleaning and monitoring. Do not try creating this type of cavity
on a tall snag, because the hollow will definitely reduce the
strength of the trunk at that section.

On the smallest scale, a snag or large tree with thick bark
can be made more attractive to some wildlife with minimal
alterations. A vertical notch gouged under the bark or outer
wood could provide a home for bats. If the cut is angled up
into the outer wood or bark, leaving a sloping roof and a
ledge at the base of the cut, a Brown Creeper could build a
nest there. You can also provide a creeper house by attaching a slab of bark to a tree to form a lean-to and holding the
lower end of the slab out with a small ledge, or with another
bark slab forming a cup (Strycker 2003). The lean-to can be
made with bark from firewood or bark found lying on the
ground.

HOLLOW LOG BOXES

Not everyone has snags or spare trees to work with, but some
people think that nest boxes are unattractive and look artificial. Besides, the best built nest box can never have the
comfy round shape or the insulation value of a natural cav-

ity in a tree. You might consider making boxes out of small log pieces. They can look more natural than rectangular nest boxes. When carefully built, they also provide better insulation.

A short section of log can be split open and partially hollowed out with hand tools to form a cavity. Hollow out the main part of the log section, but leave the upper and lower ends intact. If you split off just one-quarter or one-third of the log, it can become the front. Drill the entrance hole through it, and reattach it with hinges and a latch for monitoring and cleaning. A lid is necessary to keep rain from entering the top of the split.

The difficulty comes in mounting a log box, which is usually quite heavy. Attaching it on top of a stump can look quite natural, although moisture will eventually rot the bottom of the box. Attaching it on the trunk of a tree or snag can work well, even though it may not look quite as natural. Split or saw a little off the back of the log box to make it flat for better contact with the trunk. Drill at least two holes from

Some first attempts at hollow log boxes. The lids and bottoms allow water to get in. Old fire hose makes dandy hinges and latches.

the cavity through the back and attach the log box to the trunk with lag bolts (hex bolts).

BUILDING AND PUTTING UP NEST BOXES

In many situations, there is no opportunity for providing snags or even hollow log boxes. Nest boxes are the easiest nesting habitat to create, monitor, and clean. They can augment sparse snag habitat and help restore and expand populations of cavity nesting birds. Several excellent books are available on building and installing nest structures for every conceivable type of wildlife. See References, especially Henderson (1992), Stokes and Stokes (1994), and California Waterfowl Association (1994), and see the various websites in Organizations and Networking. Here are a few tips and reminders:

A front-opening box makes cleaning easy.

♦ Do not use wood that has been treated with preservatives, because it may give off fumes harmful to you and the birds.

♦ Try to find scrap or used wood for nest boxes. The recommended box dimensions are not precise except for the entrance hole (see below).

♦ Use materials that will stand up to harsh weather and lots of activity. Use dried lumber or exterior plywood that is at least 2 cm. (¾ in.) thick. Cedar lasts the longest in damp climates. Drywall screws work best, because nails will loosen when the wood swells and shrinks. Never use staples; they will pull out from weather and monitoring.

◆ Use a box design that suits your needs. It is easiest to clean out boxes if the front or one side swings open. However, if you will be monitoring frequently, you may prefer to open the lid. This causes less disturbance and prevents eggs or nestlings from falling out or being hidden behind the top of the swinging panel if the nest is very deep. Furthermore, lid-opening boxes can be checked later in the nesting cycle without causing early fledging. Checking side- or front-opening

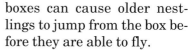

boxes can cause older nestlings to jump from the box before they are able to fly.

◆ When attaching a nest box to a live tree, remember that the tree will continue to grow. As it does, it will push the box off the trunk and engulf the nails used for attachment. It is better to use lag bolts (hex bolts) that can be loosened as the tree's diameter expands. A socket wrench makes the work easy. If you do use nails, please use only aluminum nails, which can be severed safely by a chainsaw if the tree is cut into sections sometime in the future.

◆ Use your brain as well as your brawn when putting up nest boxes. Once you are up on a ladder with the box in one hand and tools in the other, how do you hold on? Instead,

Mountain Chickadee at a lid-opening box, which can be checked without causing older nestlings to fledge early.   LaBelle

Using a rope and pulley to put up a duck nest box.   LaBelle

work with a partner. Use two ladders so one person can hold the box in place while the other uses hand tools to attach it.

♦ When putting up a huge box for ducks, have a length of rope and a nail large enough to use for a pulley. Choose the position for the box on the tree (see page 48). Then put the nail part way into the trunk above that position, or leave one branch. Tie the rope securely around the box and put the other end of the rope over the nail or branch. One person on the ground can use the nail or branch like a pulley to raise the box and hold it in place. The second person climbs the ladder, placed to one side of the box, and attaches the box to the trunk. Remove the rope and the pulley nail, or the branch if it is too close to the box.

♦ If you put up more than one box, write a number or other designation on each box. Also plot those on a map of the site (see page 127).

NEST BOX DIMENSIONS

For each species or group, the recommended diameter of the entrance hole and the minimum inside box dimensions are given. Be precise with the hole diameter, to avoid problems with non-native species. Oval holes are wider than tall. The nest boxes for each species or group can be considerably larger than the bare minimum listed. The depth of the box is measured from the inside of the lid to the floor, at the front of boxes with sloping roofs.

SPECIES / GROUP	HOLE	MINIMUM	
		DEPTH	FLOOR
Chickadees, nuthatches	3 cm. 11/8 in.	20 cm. 8 in.	10x10 cm. 4x4 in.
Wrens	3 cm. 11/8 in.	20 cm. 8 in.	8x8 cm. 3x3 in.
Bluebirds, flycatchers	4 cm. 15/8 in.	25 cm. 10 in.	10x9 cm. 4x3½ in.
Purple Martin	5½ cm. 21/8 in.	15 cm. 6 in.	15x13 cm. 6x5 in.
Other swallows	4 cm. 1½ in.	20 cm. 8 in.	10x10 cm. 4x4 in.
Wood Duck	7½x10 cm. 3x4 in.	58 cm. 23 in.	22x22 cm. 9x9 in.
Bufflehead	7½ cm. 3 in.	28 cm. 11 in.	15x15 cm. 6x6 in.
Common Merganser	10x13cm 4x5 in.	58 cm. 23 in.	22x25 cm. 9x10 in.
Other ducks	7½x10 cm. 3x4 in.	39 cm. 15 in.	20x20 cm. 8x8 in.
Kestrel, small owls	7½ cm. 3 in.	36 cm. 14 in.	15x15 cm. 6x6 in.
Barn Owl	18 cm. 7 in.	41 cm. 16 in.	41x57 cm. 16x22 in.

Western Bluebirds only
(no Mountain Bluebirds or
Ash-throated Flycatchers)
Hole 3.8 cm (1 1/2")

CHECKING A NEST BOX

You may have grown up being told that you should never touch a bird's nest, eggs, or nestlings, because the parents will never return to a nest contaminated by the smell of humans. In reality, birds have a poorly developed sense of smell, except for the vultures and a few other groups. Keen eyesight and hearing are more important to the survival of most birds, so unless the parents see or hear you examining the nest, they may not even know you were there. On the other hand, if the parents do observe your actions, which will undoubtedly look like predatory behavior, the nest could be abandoned. In most cases, quickly examining the nest and leaving right away causes only momentary alarm for the parent birds. Certain points in the nesting cycle are most vulnerable to nest abandonment:

♦   during nest building,

♦   when the female is in the nest laying an egg,

Female White-breasted Nuthatch incubating eggs in a nest box.

◆   the beginning of incubation, and

◆   the first day or two after hatching.

This section assumes that you are working with nest boxes, and that you are opening them up to examine the contents. Using a mirror and flashlight (which can be mounted on a pole) instead of opening the boxes can avoid some stress to the birds and save you some time. That is the only way you can monitor a nest in a natural cavity. However, that method cannot tell you how many eggs or hatchlings might be under a bird that sits tight in a nest.

Looking into nest boxes provides the opportunity for exciting detective work. Both during the breeding season and afterwards, you must figure out "who done it" and "what happened" in the nest box. Follow these steps (which are mostly for songbirds rather than raptors or ducks) in order to catch all the clues. There are several safety issues to be aware of, too. If the nest is active, remember to look quickly and leave, writing up your notes after you have left the nest box. Please do not check active nests in pouring rain or unseasonably cold weather, when nest abandonment often occurs.

A checklist of suggested equipment for checking nest boxes is on page 132.

The following information was compiled from our studies; publications of the North American Bluebird Society; books and articles listed in the References, especially Berger et al. (2001), Bluebird Recovery Program (1987), Bull (in press), California Waterfowl Association (1994), Pearman (2002), Scriven (1989), Sheldon (1998); and individuals listed in the Acknowledgements, especially Dave Fouts, Pat Johnston, Don McCartney, Roger Orness, Dan Varland, and Patty Vaughan.

AS YOU APPROACH EACH BOX:

1. Check the box number.

2. Look and listen for the residents before you get to the box.

♦ Yellowjackets and hornets are best noticed from a distance. If they are using the box, leave it alone! There won't be an active bird nest in it.

♦ Eggs and small nestlings of closely related species look very similar, so you must see a parent to identify them.

♦ Nestlings may make peeping sounds. If you hear them from a distance, stop and wait to see who the parents are before opening the box. If the parents notice you opening it they may stay away until you have left their nest far behind.

♦ Many parent birds will give alarm or scolding calls, or even dive at you, but some birds will perch quietly nearby and watch your actions. Take the time to look for them.

♦ Some incubating birds will look out and then drop back down into the box, although many remain quietly on the nest. Often a bird (especially the Ash-throated Flycatcher) will quietly slip out of the box, fly straight away from you using the box and tree for a screen, and hide until you have left the area. Stay alert as you approach the box.

Mountain chickadee looking out of nest box during incubation.

BEFORE YOU OPEN THE BOX:

1. Examine the ground underneath the box.

♦ An egg with a tiny puncture in it was probably removed from the nest by a House Wren (but the nest
may have been abandoned first).

♦ An infertile egg or a dead, small nestling may have
been dropped by the parent bird while carrying it
away from the nest. The egg might be whole, smashed,
or have a small puncture in it. The nestling would be
undamaged, or have skin tears with no bleeding (the
nestling died, and later the parent tore the skin while
removing it from the nest).

2. Examine the entrance hole.

Entrance hole pecked by a flicker.
LaBelle

Entrance hole chewed by a rodent.
LaBelle

♦ Spider webs across the entrance indicate a long vacancy.

♦ If the lower edge of the entrance is dirty, the box has been used (but maybe not recently).

♦ Droppings splattered on the box front below the entrance indicate large nestlings. The shallow boxes often used for swallows allow older nestlings to stick their tails out the entrance when defecating.

♦ If the entrance is enlarged, something bigger than the intended residents has been inside.

   a. If the edge has small punctures, a flicker or other bird has pecked it.

   b. If the edge has small pairs of parallel grooves, a rodent has gnawed it.

♦ Tree sap splattered on the box front all around the entrance indicates a Red-breasted Nuthatch nesting.

Red-breasted Nuthatches have splattered sap around their nest hole.

♦ One or two down feathers stuck in the entrance or on the front of a large box often mean duck eggs inside.

♦ Fresh scratches on the front or sides of the box may indicate a visit by a mammalian predator.

3. Tap on the box.

♦ Paper wasps and bumblebees, which usually do not attack, will fly out or at least buzz.

♦ Rodents will often jump out, or at least make themselves known by rustling around.

4. Take safety precautions before you open the box!

Nest box hazards include frightened birds or mammals, stinging insects, splinters, and Hanta virus carried by rodents.

♦ Protect your eyes by wearing safety goggles, dark glasses, or your prescription glasses.

♦ Protect your hands by wearing work gloves.

Please wear safety gear when checking nest boxes!   LaBelle

♦ Protect your health by wearing a dust mask as well as the glasses and gloves.

WHEN YOU OPEN THE BOX:

1. Be prepared for the sudden exit of a resident.
♦ A mouse or a wasp may wait until the box is opened before moving. An incubating bird may flush at any time during your box checking. Startling you is often their intention.

2. Peer in with your face well away from the box.
♦ A bird or chipmunk may literally fly into your face on its way out. A beetle may squirt you with acid.

3. If there is an adult bird in the box (usually a female incubating eggs):
♦ Be as quiet and quick as possible, but make no sudden motions.

♦ Keep from blocking the entrance hole (avoid the bird's perception of the box as a trap).

♦ If the bird is standing up, count eggs or nestlings and close the box.

♦ Songbirds only: If the bird is covering the nest cup, reach in slowly, stroke the bird's back, then gently push it off the cup until you can count the contents.

♦ Songbirds only: If necessary, carefully reach under the bird until its feet clutch your finger and lift it just far enough to count the contents. Then push its feet off the tip of your finger with your other fingers.

4. If there are eggs in the nest:
♦ Identify and count them.

♦ If no adult bird is or was in the box, carefully feel the eggs.

Western Bluebird eggs abandoned during cold, wet weather.

> **a.** Warm eggs are being incubated.
>
> **b.** Cold eggs may indicate an incomplete clutch, not yet being incubated (see Egg Laying on page 31).
>
> **c.** Cold eggs may indicate an abandoned clutch. Do not assume they are abandoned unless you know that at least the same number of eggs have been in the nest for more than a week.
>
> *NOTE:* A flat, clean surface of fur may hide chickadee, nuthatch, or titmouse eggs. The fur is pulled over the eggs to keep them warm whenever the female leaves the nest after each egg is laid and during incubation. Gently pull it open in the center to count and feel eggs, then replace it carefully. Similarly, a broad mass of down may have a clutch of duck eggs inside.

5. If there are egg remains in the nest, see page 96.

6. If there are live nestlings in the nest:
   ♦ Identify and count them, and note the development stage (see page 35).

Wood Duck nest of down and belly feathers, opened to show eggs.

♦ If you see blowflies or the nest is very wet, you *may* want to replace the nest (unless that would affect a research project). Keep the nestlings warm while you quickly remove the old nest and build up a layer of fresh, dry grass. Then replace the nestlings.

♦ If you are banding nestlings, only band if the skin on the legs has already hardened, but before the nestlings are old enough to fledge prematurely. This is usually nestling stage IV (see page 37).

7. If there are dead nestlings or dead adult birds in the nest:

♦ Identify, count, and examine them, and note development stage (see page 35).

♦ Dead nestlings or adults with no injuries died from abandonment, hypothermia, starvation, disease, or pesticides, but not predation.

♦ Dead nestlings having small tears with no blood, or that are outside of the nest cup, indicate death from

Nestling bluebirds that died after being abandoned during cold, wet weather.

Broken feathers in a bluebird nest raided by a chipmunk.

Nestling bluebird that died and was cleaned by insects.

abandonment, etc., and attempted removal by the parent birds.

♦ Broken feathers, torn apart carcasses, or blood on dead birds, nest, or nest box walls are indications of predation. Missing eggs or nestlings and no disturbance indicate snake predation.

♦ A fluffy mass of unbroken feathers covering an undisturbed skeleton indicates cleaning by ants or carrion beetles, rather than predation.

AS YOU REMOVE THINGS FROM THE BOX:

NOTE: **If you see rodent droppings, continue to wear dust mask, safety glasses, and gloves to avoid infection with Hanta virus!**

NOTE: **Do not remove anything from a nest that might still be active, except:**

♦ If you are sure the residents are European Starlings or House Sparrows, remove everything, including warm eggs and live nestlings. Destroy eggs and humanely kill nestlings (see page 63).

♦ If possible, remove dead nestlings or adults from a nest that is active, unless that would affect a research project. Very cold nestlings that are not able to move may not be dead, and can be revived by the parent bird brooding them.

♦ If you are uncertain of whether the nest is still active, leave it undisturbed.

1. Notice the order of layers of evidence.

♦ Check for more than one nest (but be careful not to count a nest lining as a separate nest).

♦ The topmost layer is evidence of the most recent activity.

♦ Rodents may use materials from previous nests and mix them up into their own nest.

♦ Bird droppings splattered on the walls extend down to the top edge of the nest, but that edge may be covered by a more recent nest.

2. Examine any eggs or egg remains if you are sure the nest is no longer active.

♦ Remove a nest with cold eggs *only* if you know they have remained cold for more than seven days and there are no adult birds scolding near the nest box.

♦ Songbird eggs:

a. If the eggs had hatched, the shells would have been eaten or carried away from the nest box by the parents.

b. Count and examine any unhatched eggs. To see if they were partially developed, break them on the ground. Do this well away from the nest box to prevent predators from associating the eggs with the nest box.

i. If they contain only clear liquid and/or yellow or light orange yolk, they were infertile or were abandoned at the start of incubation.

ii. If they contain dark brown, reddish, or blackish yolk or a recognizable embryo, they were chilled or abandoned after incubation had begun.

c. Eggshell fragments or eggs with a large opening and totally empty were either raided by a predator or scavenged after being abandoned. They are usually licked clean by a rodent or later scraped clean by ants.

Chickadee eggs abandoned before incubation started.

Bluebird eggs abandoned after incubation had begun.

d. A sticky or slimy part of an empty nest may be from an abandoned egg later broken by the parents when trying to remove it before starting a new nest. A really sticky part could be a bumblebee's honey cache, in which case please leave the nest alone.

♦ Duck eggs:

    a. Whitish or tan dried membranes, separate from scattered small eggshell fragments, indicate that eggs hatched. Ducks eat most of the shells but not the membranes.

    b. Unhatched, rotten eggs may explode if you crack them! Handle carefully, and break them well away from the box using a long branch or a stone. A few unhatched eggs in a successful nest (one with several membranes) were either infertile or were chilled before or during incubation. Many unhatched eggs in a nest with no membranes indicates the entire clutch was abandoned.

    c. Large sections of eggs, either with the membranes still attached or with no sign of them in the nest, indicate that the egg contents were eaten by a predator or scavenged after being abandoned.

♦ Raptor eggs:

    a. Small fragments of eggshell may indicate successfully hatched eggs. Large sections of eggs indicate that the eggs were eaten by a predator or scavenged after being abandoned.

    b. Unhatched eggs were infertile, chilled before or during incubation, or abandoned.

3. Notice any droppings or any other items in the nest or box. Wear dust mask, safety glasses, and gloves to avoid infection with Hanta virus from rodent droppings!

♦ Notice the color, size, and shape of droppings; the amount; and which layer of nest they are on.

    a. If part or all of each dropping is white (or stained pink or purple) it is from a bird.

        i. If most or all droppings are shapeless blobs they are from nestlings and often indicate that they fledged. These may be splattered

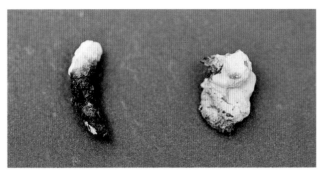

Nestling bird droppings (fecal sacs).   LaBelle

Rodent droppings (top) and adult bird droppings.

on walls, piled in corners, or may be on top of the nest and flattened by having been stepped on, sometimes forming a flat, cement-like layer.

ii. "Whitewash" covering nest, walls, and ceiling of a large box indicate American Kestrel nestlings, and usually indicate that they fledged.

iii. If most or all droppings are long and thin, often curved or coiled, they are from adults. Birds may roost in an empty box for several days if bad weather prevents foraging.

b. If droppings are dark brown or black pellets they are from a mammal. Wear dust mask, safety glasses, and gloves!

i. Droppings the shape and size of rice grains are from a mouse or chipmunk.

ii. Droppings the shape and size of small peanuts are from a squirrel or flying squirrel.

iii. A large pile of pellets soaked with urine is the winter nest of a rodent. Especially if the pile has dried out, drench nest with 10% chlorine bleach before and during removal! Avoid getting the bleach on your clothes.

iv. Droppings the size of rice grains but with the ends pointed or twisted, and often full of shiny insect remains may be from a bat.

◆ Cast pellets (undigested bones, fur, and feathers regurgitated by raptors) indicate an owl or kestrel roosted or started to nest. *NOTE*: The nest or roost could still be active.

◆ Dead rodents, small fish, or other prey items in a large box indicate a raptor nest start, which could still be active.

◆ Dead insects or other food items in a fledged songbird nest were dropped by nestlings.

◆ Dead insects, etc. on top of a songbird nest with dead nestlings were probably brought in when weather improved after a bad period, but nestlings were too weak to eat.

◆ One or a few feathers dropped, rather than built into a nest, usually indicate a bird roosted in the box. Usually there are adult droppings, too.

◆ Lots of down feathers and small curved feathers indicate that a duck laid eggs. The female pulls these from her belly after she has laid most of the clutch.

Western Screech-Owl pellets of rodent fur and bones.   LaBelle

Grasshoppers dropped in a fledged bluebird nest.

Some of the feathers can be saved for species identification, if necessary.

♦ Large, wide, curved feathers indicate a Tree or Violet-green Swallow nested, particularly in colder climate areas. They add only a few feathers before beginning to incubate the eggs. By hatching time there may be more than 100 feathers.

Bumblebee nest in an old Northern Flying Squirrel nest.

♦ Grape-sized hollow chambers lined with yellowish wax built into an abandoned bird or rodent nest are the nest of a bumblebee.

♦ If there is no nest but there are droppings in the box, they indicate it was used for roosting or sheltering in rainy weather rather than nesting.

♦ If there is no nest but there are food items in the box, they may indicate it was used for food storage.

   a. Dried truffles or mushrooms were collected by a Northern Flying Squirrel.

   b. Seeds and dried flowers were collected by a mouse.

4. Notice the present shape of the nest. Perfect cup indicates the nest was not used, was not successful, or has just been built.

♦ Very deep, perfect cup with vertical sides may indicate that egg laying was delayed and adults just kept adding nest material. This is usually the result of bad weather.

Truffles stored by Northern Flying Squirrel.

◆ Packed down, flattened out, or flat-bottomed cup indicates that nestlings grew large, bounced around
while building up wing muscles and begging for food,
and *usually* indicates they fledged.

◆ Disturbed nest, especially if partially pulled up to entrance hole, indicates predation. Nestlings often clutch
nest material when pulled from nest.

◆ Absolutely flat, clean surface of fur or tiny feathers
covers the eggs of a chickadee or nuthatch before and
during incubation. A flat mass of down and small
feathers covers duck eggs during incubation. Carefully search for eggs. Do *not* remove the nest if it might
still be active.

◆ Very wide cup with sloping sides, and no droppings,
usually indicates use by rodents for raising their
young (see Key to the Nests of Secondary Cavity Nesters, page 111).

◆ Bird nest subtly rearranged to form a smaller hole in
the center of the cup leading down to a larger hollow
was taken over by rodents.

Fledged bluebird nest (LaBelle). Warm weather makes the nestlings active, so the whole nest gets flattened. When they are big enough, the nestlings perch in the entrance hole to be fed, preventing the parents from entering the box to remove the droppings. A warm weather fledged nest is very flat and covered with droppings.

Fledged bluebird nest. Cold weather makes the nestlings huddle together in the middle of the nest, so only the center of the nest gets flattened. The parents are able to enter the box to remove most of the droppings. A cold weather fledged nest is not very flat and has few or no droppings.

5. Notice the nest materials used in each layer, their length, and the style of nest building.

♦ See Key to the Nests of Secondary Cavity Nesters on page 111.

6. Examine underneath the nest.

♦ Feather dandruff indicates that nestlings survived at least until they were mostly feathered, and often indicates that the nest successfully fledged. Be careful in distinguishing between dust and the curved pieces of the keratin feather sheaths. Rub some between your thumb and forefinger. Dust feels slightly gritty, while feather dandruff feels slippery like soap flakes or talcum powder.

Feather dandruff filters to the bottom of the nest, making box cleaning very dusty work.   LaBelle

Bluebird nest turned upside-down to show blowfly pupae.   LaBelle

♦ Small, gray grubs or shiny reddish brown pupae under the nest are blowflies (see page 73).

7. Examine the walls, ceiling, and floor of the box.

♦ Flickers and possibly other woodpeckers peck on the
  walls, carving out hollows in them, especially when
  cramped in a small box.

♦ Northern Flying Squirrels and possibly other rodents
  gnaw on all the inside surfaces, carving out hollows
  in them, especially when cramped in a small box.

♦ "Whitewash" on inside surfaces indicates there were
  bird nestlings (see bird droppings, pages 35 and 38).

AFTER YOU EXAMINE ALL THE EVIDENCE:

**1. If the nest is no longer active, clean the nest box
thoroughly.**

♦ If there are rodent droppings, wear dust mask, safety
  glasses, and gloves. Keep dampening the nest with
  10% chlorine bleach to reduce dust that could include
  Hanta virus.

◆ Remove all nest material. Do not leave any evidence to confuse you later. Some birds will not re-use a box with an old nest in it, even for a second nest, particularly in areas with many nest parasites.

   a. Scrape all droppings off the nest box walls and entrance. A putty knife is useful.

   b. Scoop up or sweep out all dandruff and egg fragments.

   c. Remove all down feathers from nest box floor, walls, and entrance.

◆ **NOTE**: Do not clean out the nest box if there is a new nest start on top, or if adults are near the nest box carrying nest material. However, if the nest is very wet, or there are dead birds or blowflies, you might set the new nest aside and replace it after cleaning out the box as above.

◆ Dispose of (preferably bury) unhatched eggs or dead birds away from the nest box, to avoid alerting predators to associate the box with a potential food source.

◆ During fall box cleaning, paper wasps that winter in old nests can be scooped out safely.

◆ If ladybugs are in the nest box in the fall, please leave these helpful predators of garden insects to spend the winter in your box. If there is an old nest, clean it out in early spring, after the ladybugs have left.

2. Consider all of the evidence you have observed:
   ◆ A songbird nest should be considered successful only if:

      a. the nest or at least the bottom of the cup is flattened, and

      b. there is a moderate or abundant amount of dandruff underneath, and

      c. there are fewer than three dead nestlings, and

      d. there are at least a few droppings (except for House Wrens).

Fledged Purple Martin nest with one dead nestling.

♦ A duck nest should be considered successful only if:

   a. there are one or more egg membranes present.

♦ A raptor nest should be considered successful only if:

   a. the nest scrape is packed hard and flat (except rounded up in the corners), and

   b. there is a moderate (owls) or abundant (kestrel) amount of droppings and whitewash on the inside walls of the nest box or around the nest, and

   c. there are food remains or cast pellets in the nest or on the ground under the nest box.

♦ By separating layers found in a nest box, often two or three different nests can be discerned. Identifying them is usually possible, but figuring out the fate of each is difficult.

   a. Dandruff from a nest filters all the way to the bottom of the box, unless stopped by a cement-like layer of droppings in a previous fledged nest.

♦ When one species modifies the nest of a previous occupant, rather than covering it with a new nest, even

Egg membranes in a successful
Wood Duck nest.

Droppings cover the inside of a box
with a successful kestrel nest.

distinguishing mammal vs. bird is challenging (see
Key to the Nests of Secondary Cavity Nesters on page
111).

a. A nest made of both short and long pieces of commonly used materials may indicate that a bird
built the nest, and later a rodent modified it by
chewing the long pieces into short ones, often
all the same length.

b. On the other hand, occasionally a bird adds only
a few long pieces to a nest that a rodent built.

c. A rodent may completely stir up several layers
of nest materials into its own style of nest. A
duck may mix old nest material and wood chips
into its down and feather nest.

The fledged upper nest was removed to show dandruff on the
layer of droppings of the fledged first nest. Both were bluebird nests.

A successful chipmunk nest on top of a fledged bluebird nest.

The more often you check a box during the breeding season
and keep good notes, the less confusion you will have in your
detective work!

KEY TO NESTS OF SECONDARY CAVITY NESTERS

This key is to help you identify nests commonly found in nest boxes in the western United States and Canada. It uses information in Ehrlich et al. (1988) and Harrison (1978). For further help, check these and other books listed in the References, especially Baicich and Harrison (1997) and Harrison (1979). Also check the websites in Organizations and Networking.

Unless the residents were seen at the box during the breeding season, many nests can only be identified to group or genus, not to species. The size of the open cup fits the size of the species that made it and is an identification clue. Several groups appear in more than one place in the key, because they employ more than one style or dominant material. Various rodent nests are also included because they can look like bird nests and they are commonly found in nest boxes.

The descriptions are of nests as they look when first built, during egg laying or incubation, or when nestlings are small. When you examine a nest after youngsters have bounced around in it, you may have to be imaginative in reconstructing its original shape.

The key describes single nests. However, if a nest was modified by a second species, rather than just covered up when another nest was built later, you will need to use clues from several of the descriptions below.

When you find a nest made of some bizarre material, remember that secondary cavity nesting species are opportunistic and inventive. Usually the weird stuff closely resembles, in color or texture, some commonly used material. If wood shavings are incorporated into a nest, don't forget that they may have been put there by people (maybe even you). The style of nest building may be most helpful in your identification.

1. A. SMALL NEST. Cup or hollow is less than 8 cm. (3 in.) in diameter, built in a small nest box (occasionally in a large box) .... Go to 2

1. B. LARGE NEST. Cup or hollow is greater than 10 cm. (4 in.) in diameter, built in a larger nest box. .... Go to 9

2. A. Sap from conifers smeared or splattered around entrance hole .... **Red-breasted Nuthatch**

2. B. No sap around hole .... Go to 3

3. A. Nest is an open cup or a loose mass of materials .... Go to 4

3. B. Nest is a hollow ball or has a flat coverlet hiding an open cup .... Go to 7

4. A. Cup or loose mass with pieces of material that are at least 5 cm. (2 in.) long .... Go to 5

4. B. Cup made of short pieces of material, less than 2 cm. (3/4 in.) .... Go to 6

5. A. Nest is a cup with some long pieces of material wound in a circle:

- ◆ *Grass* in a neat cup, often using just one species of grass, with maybe a few feathers or strings carefully incorporated .... **bluebird**

- ◆ *Grass* in a loose, small cup (often several very long pieces used), usually with large curved feathers stuck with the shafts down to arch over the cup .... **swallow**

- ◆ *Grass* mixed with, or with a lining of, fur, hair, feathers, rootlets, finely shredded bark, moss, etc. in a small, neat cup .... **nuthatch, chickadee, or titmouse**

- ◆ *Grass* mixed with coarse materials in a messy nest with a large cup .... **European Starling**

- ◆ *Grass* mixed loosely with feathers, trash, etc. in a huge, messy nest with material arched over the top

Tree Swallow nest, side view.

White-breasted Nuthatch nest.

Oak titmouse nest.

of the small cup to form a short tube with a hole at the side nearest the box entrance (Pamela Johnston from Oregon described one nest as containing "relatively loathsome objects like a used coffee filter and cigarette filters") . . . . **House Sparrow**

◆   *Twigs* in a large mass, with a tiny, neat cup of fur, long hair or feathers, usually in one back corner . . . . **House Wren**

◆   *Twigs* in a tiny platform nest glued to the walls of a huge box . . . . **Vaux's Swift**

◆   *Moss* mixed loosely with leaves, twigs, feathers, fur, and snakeskins forming a messy heap with a deep but tiny cup, which is often in one back corner . . . . **Bewick's Wren**

◆   *Bark* strips (especially juniper) curved into a neat cup . . . . **bluebird**

◆   *Bark* chunks and moss as a base, with a lining of fur, feathers, rootlets, or anything fuzzy (Pat Johnston of the Prescott Bluebird Recovery Project described a nuthatch nest as looking like "what you'd dump out of the vacuum cleaner.") . . . . **nuthatch**

5. B. Nest is a loose mass with some long or large pieces of material:

◆   *Green leaves*, coarse grass stalks, twigs, shell pieces, etc. in a loose mass with a slight cup. May have a mud sill built across the cavity between the entrance and the nest (the sill may function to keep young nestlings back from the entrance and to shade them, according to Dave Fouts, Purple Martin expert from Oregon) . . . . **Purple Martin**

◆   *Dead leaves, twigs*, moss, lichen, and/or other materials in a loose mass with a poorly defined hollow. Nest start . . . . **squirrel or Northern Flying Squirrel**

Side view of a House
Sparrow nest.
                    LaBelle

Purple Martin nest - Looking down into an abandoned nest that has been removed
from a nest box. The eggs were laid in the back of the box (right side). A sill or
berm of mud was built up on the front edge of the nest, nearest to the entrance.

6. Nest cup has wads of short pieces of material:

 ♦ *Moss* as a base, with fur, hair, feathers, fine strips of soft bark, or thistle down lining a small cup
.... **chickadee, nuthatch, or titmouse**

 ♦ *Fur* nest, made of tiny tufts from pulled apart coyote scats and owl pellets, with a small, neat cup
.... Mountain Chickadee or nuthatch

 ♦ *Fur* and/or coarse hair nest, made of large clumps, often using whole coyote scats, owl pellets, coarse grass, and matted bunches of cow, elk, or deer hair, with a large cup. It may also have dried cow manure at the bottom .... **Ash-throated Flycatcher**

 ♦ *Grass, lichen, and/or moss*, chewed short pieces all mixed up into a ball with a wide cup pushed out from the middle by active babies ..... **chipmunk**

7. A. Nest is a hollow ball with a small hole at the top
.... Go to 8

7. B. Nest has a flat coverlet of fur or small feathers on top, hiding a small cup of fur, feathers, grass, or moss
.... **chickadee or nuthatch**

(Note: Make sure it is not unhatched eggs in a fledged nest, with the cup packed down flat, feather dandruff underneath, and usually at least a few droppings on top.)

8. Nest is a hollow ball with a small hole, usually at the top:

 ♦ *Twigs* filling a small nest box to the ceiling, with a slight tunnel from the box entrance over the top and down to the tiny, neat cup of fur, hair or feathers which is in a hollow in a back corner of the box
.... **House Wren**

 ♦ *Grass* chewed into small pieces, mixed with fine rootlets, thistle down, or other materials in a hollow ball
.... **chipmunk or mouse**

 ♦ *Moss* mixed loosely with dead leaves and twigs in a large hollow ball .... **squirrel**

Top: Looking down into a box with a House Wren stick nest lined with feathers.
Lower left: Ash-throated Flycatcher nest of deer hair, grass, and baling twine.
Lower right: Chestnut-backed Chickadee nestlings (Stage IV) in moss and fur nest.

♦ *Moss* mostly of a single kind (usually a coarse type with large leaf tufts) in a large hollow ball .. **Northern Flying Squirrel, Douglas Squirrel**

♦ *Lichen* (black or gray/green "old man's beard") in a large, hollow ball, sometimes with a few twigs included . . . . **Northern Flying Squirrel**

♦ *Bark* (often from western red cedar) finely shredded and chewed into a woolly, hollow ball .. **Northern Flying Squirrel, mouse, chipmunk**

♦ *Downy seed parachutes* of thistle, fireweed, or milkweed in a hollow ball . . . . **mouse**

9. A. Nest is a large mass of added materials:

♦ *Down and very small, curved belly feathers,* usually mixed with wood chips in a loose mass or large cup (Note: Save some of the belly feathers to match with study skins and mounted birds at museums if you did not see what species used the nest box) .. **Wood Duck, Hooded Merganser, other duck**

♦ *Lichen* (black or gray/green "old man's beard") in a large hollow ball, or a wide cup pushed out by active babies . . . . **Northern Flying Squirrel**

♦ *Moss, leaves, twigs*, etc. in a large hollow ball, or a wide cup pushed out by active babies . . . . **squirrel**

9. B. Nest is a bowl-shaped dent in wood chips, with few or no additions:

♦ *Large dent* in top of packed down wood chips (or the top of a previous rodent or bird nest.) Roost or nest start . . . . **duck, American Kestrel, or owl**

♦ *Raptor pellets and remains of prey items* around a dent. Roost or nest start. . . . . **American Kestrel or owl**

♦ ***Dead rodents, fish, or other food items*** stashed around a dent Nest start . . . .
. . . . **American Kestrel or owl**

Top: Newborn Northern Flying Squirrels in a lichen nest that has been slightly opened.
Lower left: Mouse nest (removed from a nest box) made of plant seed down, with an old hornet's nest for an air mattress.
Lower right: Front view of a Fox Squirrel nest (LaBelle).

Hooded Merganser nest that fledged a few ducklings.

American Kestrel nest and eggs. LaBelle

Western Screech-Owl nestlings, with feathers from birds that were fed to them.

MONITORING NEST BOXES

Although it is possible to look into many natural cavities to monitor nests by using a mirror and light, properly designed nest boxes make monitoring much easier. As a general rule, the more often you check nest boxes, and the more boxes you monitor, the more information you can obtain. On the other hand, practical considerations may limit both the frequency of your visits and the size of your project. Watching a couple of nest boxes in the back yard is a whole different proposition than monitoring 300 boxes scattered around 10 sites which are a four-hour drive from your home. But even the simplest box monitoring program is research – a study of secondary cavity nesting birds. As such, it should be planned carefully, conducted consistently, and documented thoroughly. Monitoring, by definition, is a long-term study. The continuity is the most critical element, and your planning must provide consistency over many years.

SETTING OBJECTIVES

Why put up nest boxes? Why check them? As you plan your project, you should ask yourself what it is that you want to accomplish. Is the main reason for the project to provide educational experiences for kids? To help native wildlife? Is there a particular species or group of species you are most interested in studying? A certain habitat type? An individual piece of land on which you want to monitor birds? Or diversify habitat?

Even though your objectives may change later on, it is essential that you think them out as a preliminary step to your planning. If your objective is simply to provide some good, fun work and obtain whatever data you can, that is fine. But if you want to track long-term population trends of certain species, you must make sure that your study design will provide sufficient data to be statistically valid. A lack of clear objectives too often leads to a lack of commitment, and a great opportunity may fizzle out.

PLANNING THE PROJECT

Basing your decisions on your written objectives, you should specify what tasks are involved and who will accomplish each. This is the time to decide on the scope and scale of the project and the level of commitment of each participant. Make sure that the size and intensity of your study are reasonable given your budget and the time commitment of each member of your team. In the long run, a small scale and well-organized project yielding regular data is more valuable than sporadic data from a larger but less systematic effort.

After you have considered your objectives, the three main questions to address are the location of the study site, the number of nest boxes, and the intensity of your monitoring schedule.

SITE LOCATION

Frequently, the location of the study is pre-determined – you are monitoring a particular piece of land. If you do have some choice, the following considerations may be helpful.

♦   The more convenient your access to the site, the more often you may be able to visit it.

♦   If you are interested in a particular species, find the best available habitat. If possible, ascertain whether or not the species occurs on the site before you place your boxes.

♦   The most valuable nest box monitoring would track all secondary cavity nesting species occurring in a particular habitat type. However, some species only occasionally use nest boxes, or occur at very low population densities, so be realistic in your expectations.

♦ Visit the site frequently before putting up boxes, and make a list of the species seen and heard during all seasons.

NUMBER OF NEST BOXES TO MONITOR

Although it is difficult to predict, the number of nests you hope to monitor should determine the number of boxes you place. Even with careful attention to the design, habitat, and placement of nest boxes, not all of them will be used by birds, and fewer by any single species. A good rule of thumb is to figure that half of the nest boxes will not be used by any birds at all. If you are lucky, or you put up boxes in excellent habitat for species that commonly use boxes, you may approach 100 percent utilization. Consider the following factors in your project planning:

♦ The fewer boxes you put up, the greater your chance of monitoring them frequently and consistently.

♦ The more boxes you put up, the greater your chance of obtaining sufficient data to meet your objectives.

♦ Very few of the boxes may be used by birds (especially ducks and flycatchers) for the first year or two,

Tree Swallow study site with nest boxes in a grid pattern.

probably because the boxes are viewed as alien objects rather than cavities in the trees.

♦ Some boxes may need to be relocated after the first year or two to find the best locations and increase the occupancy rate, particularly by the less common species.

♦ With chickadees and probably owls and some other species, the boxes may need to be moved slightly every three or four years to maintain a high occupancy rate.

♦ If you are comparing sites or habitats, either standardize the number of nest boxes per site or keep adding boxes until you can standardize the number of boxes used for nesting, or used by a particular species.

Make sure that you put up enough boxes to continue obtaining a meaningful amount of data. In an intensive research project, you may need to have at least ten active nests on each of ten study sites in order to have sufficient statistical rigor. At the other extreme, you only need to have a single nest in your one box in order to participate in Cornell's national Birdhouse Network (see page 135).

For monitoring regional population trends of individual species or groups, you should keep adding and relocating boxes until you annually get at least 20 nests of each species that commonly occurs in the area and habitat, and that commonly uses nest boxes. That will generally mean 20 nests each of Wood Duck, Hooded Merganser, House Wren, maybe American Kestrel, or any species of chickadees, bluebirds, or swallows. The other species less frequently use nest boxes, being more apt to excavate their own nests or to use natural tree cavities. Unless you are very lucky, or monitor a huge number of boxes, you are unlikely to have more than a few owls, swifts, flycatchers, or nuthatches using the boxes in your project. For most general monitoring efforts, 50 nest boxes in one habitat type may be adequate. Focus on the common species, but try to entice reluctant box occupants, be patient,

Be patient. When your nest boxes have been up for a few years they may start to attract some less common species. Top: Barrow's Goldeneye female and ducklings. Lower left: Northern Saw-whet Owl, a fairly common species but rarely seen in the daylight. Lower right: Ash-throated Flycatcher near its nest in a woodpecker hole (LaBelle).

Bufflehead female. This species rarely uses nest boxes except in Canada. It prefers small cavities or hollow log boxes.

Bewick's Wren is another species that rarely uses nest boxes.
LaBelle

Finding a Pacific Treefrog resting in a nest box is a rare but fun surprise.
LaBelle

Students monitoring bluebird nest boxes and writing notes.

and just be happy with whatever you get for the rare ones. Pooling the efforts of several monitoring projects may be the only way that the breeding productivity of these less common species can be monitored. This is one of the best reasons for joining the national networks (see page 135).

Particularly in a research project, or wherever you put up a large number of boxes, it is essential to make a map of the box locations. Vegetation growth and changing seasons modify the way a site looks and can obscure previously conspicuous boxes. Plotting locations on a map is an excellent project for students. Use a GPS (Global Positioning System) unit and download to a mapping program, or plot the boxes by hand on an enlarged section of a topographic map or aerial photo.

NUMBER OF VISITS

How often you monitor your nest boxes depends on several factors, including budget constraints, time and travel distance to reach the project site, and the species being monitored. Three different levels of monitoring intensity are described here, based on the frequency and timing of visits. Simply checking and cleaning the boxes once a year after the breeding season is not recommended, but is certainly far better than not checking them at all.

Level I Monitoring

♦ Breeding season visits, to identify species:

One visit during the early part of the season
One or two visits during later part of theseason

♦ Post-breeding visit, to determine nest outcomes and to repair or relocate boxes

Level II Monitoring

♦ Breeding season visits, to identify species and determine nest outcomes:

Two to four visits per month (every seven to 14 days) during the entire season or the major portion of it

♦ Post-breeding visit, to determine outcome of late nests and to repair or relocate boxes

Level III Monitoring

♦ Breeding season visits, to identify species and determine nest outcomes:

Two visits per week (every three to four days) during the entire season

♦ Post-breeding visit, to repair or relocate boxes

Level I Monitoring works well for cavity nesting ducks, raptors, swifts, remote sites, and zero budgets. To be effective, however, it requires close monitoring of weather conditions, considerable knowledge of nesting-cycle timing of the species, keen detective work, and a larger dose of luck than the other levels. Species and clutch size can be determined on the first visit, which should be planned to occur during incubation. The focus of the second visit is to determine hatch rate or number of nestlings surviving and ready to fledge, and to identify species for late nests. A third visit can be timed to determine number of surviving nestlings for late or second nests. The exact number of fledglings can only rarely be determined. Nest outcomes determined in late summer or fall are often muddled by the manipulations of ants or rodents.

Level II Monitoring works well for most species, including raptors, bluebirds, chickadees, swallows, and flycatchers. Ideally, nests are checked during the egg-laying, incubation, and nestling phases, and right after fledging. Although some phases will be missed on many nests, nest outcome, clutch size, and number of fledglings usually can be determined. If visits are made only during the major portion of the breeding season, key information from the earliest and latest nests will also be missed, as well as some entire nests. Closer timing (every seven to 10 days) may be needed for wrens, which have a shorter nesting cycle. Less frequent visits (14 days or even longer) are best for the owls and kestrels, which have a longer nesting cycle. On some of the visits, or occasional extra visits, you can use a light and mirror or use binoculars from a distance to quickly determine when eggs have hatched or nestlings have fledged.

Students putting up nest boxes and mapping the locations.   LaBelle

Western Screech-Owl nestling being weighed, after being marked with a numbered leg band.

Level III Monitoring provides more consistent data than the other levels, and is essential to many research projects on songbirds. It is not appropriate for ducks (because the ducklings leave the nest right away), and the frequency of visits could harass ducks, owls, kestrels, swifts, and flycatchers into abandoning nests. Clutch size, hatch rate, and the number of fledglings usually can be determined. Length of incubation and nestling period can be determined or closely estimated. Timing of visits to coincide with particular nest phases can assure obtaining precise data, but requires flexibility of schedule and a major commitment of time and effort. Use of a mirror and light mounted on a pole can save a lot of time during most monitoring visits. Closer monitoring of all phases of the nesting cycle of individual nests is possible at this level. This can help prevent nest abandonment or early fledging, which occasionally can be problems with the other levels because the timing of visits may coincide with vulnerable periods for some nests.

RECORDING NEST DATA

The importance of collecting data consistently cannot be overstated. It is fine to use a pocket notepad and your own abbreviations or codes while you are actually out checking boxes. However, it is imperative to then fill out a datasheet or enter your records into a computer database at the end of each site visit or each day. Use a data sheet printed from one of the networking groups via its website (see page 135), or create a form to suit your study. Better still, you can contribute your records directly to one of the networks.

On each visit, you should record the following data for each nest box, depending on the stage in the nesting cycle (see page 27):

◆ the date and year

◆ the site name and nest box number (or other designation)

◆ species (if no adults are seen, describe the nest and contents for later identification)

◆ number of eggs, and whether they are warm (being incubated) or cold (partial clutch or abandoned)

◆ number and development stage of nestlings (see page 35)

◆ number, development stage, and condition of any dead birds

◆ amount and identity of any droppings or food items

◆ condition of the nest (new and clean, flattened and dirty, dandruff underneath, etc.)

◆ signs of predation (partly pulled up toward entrance hole, broken feathers, fresh scratches around entrance hole, etc.)

See Checking a Nest Box for more details.

EQUIPMENT CHECKLIST

This list is all-inclusive. Choose the items that apply to your project. Wear sturdy footwear and clothes you do not mind getting dirty. Raingear is often useful for working in wet brush, but checking active nests in heavy rain or unseasonably cold weather causes unnecessary distress to nesting birds, and ladders may become dangerously slippery.

Putting up, repairing, or relocating boxes:

Day pack, food, water, and weather protection
Work gloves
First aid kit (including bee sting kit. eyewash, tweezers)
Map of the site, GPS unit, and/or compass
Marking pens
Notebook and data sheets
Pens or pencils
Ladders (one or two)
Pruning saws and loppers
Nest boxes
Wire cutters, nails, or other fastenings, pry bar
Lag bolts and socket wrenches
Hammer and nails (aluminum)
Screw drivers and screws
Wood chips (in plastic bags, each with enough for one box)
Rope and pulley nails for large boxes

Checking and cleaning boxes:

Day pack, food, water, and weather protection
Work gloves
First aid kit (including bee sting kit, eyewash, tweezers)
Dust masks
Safety glasses
Map of the site, GPS unit, and/or compass
Binoculars
Notebook and data sheets
Pens or pencils
Ladders
Screwdriver, if needed to open boxes
Spray bottle of 10 percent bleach
Putty knife
Wood chips (in plastic bags, each with enough for one box)
Wire, etc. for emergency box repairs
Plastic bags or film cans for down feather samples
Marking pens or extra notebook paper to mark samples
Calipers for measuring abandoned eggs
Permits if you will be handling protected species
Mirror, pole, flashlight, extra batteries
Camera
Live trap for starlings or House Sparrows

ADDITIONAL SOURCES OF INFORMATION

PERMITS

In general, you may not need any permits just to look in nest boxes if you do not handle the nestlings, or to clean out nests after the birds have left. You *are required* to have a permit if you rescue orphaned nestlings either to hand raise them or to cross-foster them into another nest with similar aged nestlings. You are also required to have a permit to keep old nests and unhatched eggs, dead migratory birds, and even feathers found in nests. You should check with your state or provincial wildlife agency before you start up a nest box program, because regulations are not the same in every state and province. See Fish and Wildlife Agencies, below. If you plan to band or color mark any birds for your research, you must have *both* a U. S. Fish and Wildlife Service banding permit and a state permit. If in Canada, you need *both* Canadian Wildlife Service and provincial permits. In either country you will need several months of lead time to secure the permits. You do *not* need any permit to remove House Sparrow and European Starling nests, eggs, or nestlings, or to kill the adults of these introduced species.

ORGANIZATIONS AND NETWORKING

It is usually much easier to find the time to go out in the field and collect data than it is to analyze it. However, information that is stuck on a shelf or tucked away in your computer is as good as useless. Do something with it. Analyze it, publish it, and at least share it with one or more of the organizations listed below. Your individually modest contribution of data can become a goldmine when combined with other monitoring efforts. There are several national and regional networks to plug into, and you can always publish your own study later on. Some of these organizations specialize in one group of species, but all are places to turn to when you want basic information on nest box design or you need help with a particular problem.

Fish and wildlife agencies – Each agency has an office or division for the non-hunted species. They may add your nest records to their wildlife database. They may require that you have a permit to monitor nest boxes, and definitely do require a permit to band birds.

> **U. S. Fish and Wildlife Service**, check phone directory for local office in your region.
>
> **Bird Banding Laboratory**, USGS Patuxent Wildlife Research Center, 12100 Beech Forest Rd., Laurel, MD 20708-4037. BBL@usgs.gov
>
> **Canadian Wildlife Service**, check phone directory for local office in your province. Also, Bird Banding Office, Canadian Wildlife Service, 1125 Colonel By Dr., Ottawa, Ontario K1A 0H3. The BBO e-mail is cws@ec.gc.ca
>
> **California Department of Fish and Game**, 1416 Ninth St., Sacramento, CA 95814. www.dfg.ca.gov
>
> **Oregon Department of Fish and Wildlife**, Wildlife Division, 3406 Cherry Ave. NE, Salem, OR 97303-4924. www.dfw.state.or.us
>
> **Washington Department of Fish and Wildlife**, 600 Capitol Way North, Olympia, WA 98501-1091. www.wa.gov/wdfw
>
> **Idaho Department of Fish and Game**, 600 S. Walnut, PO Box 25, Boise, ID 83707. www.state.id.us/fishgame
>
> **British Columbia Conservation Data Centre**, Ministry of Sustainable Resource Management, PO Box 9993 Stn. Prov. Govt., Victoria, BC V8W 9R7. http://srmwww.gov.bc.ca/cdc

Partners In Flight (PIF) – The coordinating program for the study and conservation of landbirds including Neotropical migrant species. It has prepared protocols for several standardized bird study methods. The OR/WA Chapter has written habitat conservation plans for five ecoregions.
www.partnersinflight.org

American Bird Conservancy – A nonprofit group that publishes *Bird Conservation*, makes small grants available for research, and provides a home base for PIF. 4249 Loudoun Ave., PO Box 249, The Plains, VA 20198. www.abcbirds.org

Cornell Laboratory of Ornithology – A membership institute associated with Cornell University. It publishes a newsletter and information leaflets, and coordinates The Birdhouse Network (TBN) and several other nationwide citizen science projects. They encourage you to send them your nest box data, either electronically or on their data form. 159 Sapsucker Woods Road, Ithaca, NY 14850-1999. http://birds.cornell.edu/birdhouse

North American Bluebird Society – A nonprofit group that publishes *Bluebird* and educational brochures, maintains a database of nest box use, and makes small grants available for research on cavity nesting species. They encourage you to send them your nest box data, either electronically or on their data form. PO Box 74, Darlington, WI 53530. www.nabluebirdsociety.org

Bluebird Recovery Program of the Audubon Chapter of Minneapolis – A nonprofit group that publishes educational brochures, maintains a database of nest box use, and makes small grants available for research on bluebirds. PO Box 3801, Minneapolis, MN 55403. www.geocities.com/RainForest/5835

Purple Martin Conservation Association – A nonprofit group that publishes the *Purple Martin Update* and educational brochures and makes small grants available for research on martins. Edinboro University of Pennsylvania, Edinboro, PA 16444. www.purplemartin.org

California Waterfowl Association – A nonprofit group that publishes an educational booklet. 4630 Northgate Blvd., Suite 150, Sacramento, CA 95834. www.calwaterfowl.org

Driftwood Wildlife Association – A nonprofit group that publishes *Chaetura* and conducts research on Chimney Swifts. 1206 West 38th St., Suite 1105, Austin, TX 78705. DWA@concentric.net

Bat Conservation International – A nonprofit group that publishes educational brochures. PO Box 162603, Austin, TX 78716. www.batcon.org

Frontier Tree & Wildlife – A company that specializes in snag creation for wildlife, and conducts workshops and training. PO Box 6252, Bellevue, WA 98008.

REFERENCES

Aber, J., R. P. Neilson, and S. McNulty. 2001. Forest processes and global environmental change: Predicting the effects of individual and multiple stressors. *BioScience* 51(9):735-751.

Baicich, P. J. and C. J. O. Harrison. 1997. *A Guide to the Nests, Eggs, and Nestlings of NorthAmerican Birds*. Academic Press, San Diego, CA.

Bateman, H. 2001. Boreal Owls: Habitat preferences for artificial nest boxes. *Bluebird* 23(4): 12-13.

Berger, C., K. Kridler, and J. Griggs. 2001. *The Bluebird Monitor's Guide*. Harper Collins, New York, NY.

Bermudez, B. 2002. Sparrow, starling competition with Eastern Bluebirds: Is the answer larger holes? *Bluebird* 24(2):8-11.

Bluebird Recovery Program. 1987. Predators and problems on the bluebird trail. (educational leaflet). Bluebird Recovery Committee of the Audubon Chapter of Minneapolis, Minneapolis, MN.

Brown, D. 2002. Pennsylvania bluebird project studies several pairing choices. *Bluebird* 24(3): 6-9.

Brown, E. R. 1985. Management of wildlife and fish habitats in forests of Western Oregon and Washington. Publication No.: R6-F&WL-192-1985. USDA Forest Service, Portland, OR.

Brown, T. K. 2000. Ecology and maintenance or wildlife trees and logs. Joint Conference of Society for Northwestern Vertebrate Biology and The Wildlife Society Washington Chapter, Mar. 15-17, 2000, Ocean Shores, WA.

Bull, E. L., C. G. Parks, and T. R. Torgersen. 1997. Trees and logs important to wildlife in the interior Columbia River basin. PNW-GTR-390. USDA Forest Service, Portland, OR.

Bull, E. L. 2002. Vaux's Swifts continue to use nest boxes. *Chaetura* 7(1):1.

Bull, E. L. 2003. Use of nest boxes by Vaux's Swifts. *Journal of Field Ornithology 74(4): 394-400*.

California Waterfowl Association. 1994. *A Guide to Installing and Managing Wood Duck Boxes*. California Waterfowl Association, Sacramento, CA.

Campbell, S. 1984. *The Complete Book of Birdhouse Construction for Woodworkers*. Dover Press, New York, NY.

Davis, W. H., P. J. Kalisz, and J. Powell. 2001. Kentucky Study: Cavity-entrance orientation and nest-site selection is discussed. *Bluebird* 23(3):10-11.

Davis, W. H. and P. Roca. 1995. *Bluebirds and Their Survival*. University Press of Kentucky, Lexington, KY.

Dhondt, A. A. and T. Phillips. 2001. A question of preference. *Birdscope* 15(2):1-3.

Dillingham, C. P., S. P. Cross, and P. W. Dillingham. 2003. Two environmental factors that influence usage of bat houses in managed forests of southwestern Oregon. *Northwestern Naturalist* 84:20-23.

Ehrlich, P. R., D. S. Dobkin, and D. Wheye. 1988. *The Birder's Handbook: A Field Guide to the Natural History of North American Birds*. Simon and Schuster, Inc., New York, NY.

Elbroch, M. with E. Marks. 2001. *Bird Tracks and Sign: A Guide to North American Species*. Stackpole Books, Mechanicsburg, PA.

Eltzroth, E. K. 2000. Bluebird deaths in Oregon examined. *Bluebird* 22(3):16-17.

Evans, M. R., D. B. Lank, W. S. Boyd, and F. Cooke. 2002. A comparison of the characteristics and fate of Barrow's goldeneye and bufflehead nests in nest boxes and natural cavities. *The Condor* 104:610-619.

Fouts, D. R. 1996. Ten years helping Purple Martins in the Pacific Northwest. *Purple Martin Update* 7(1):7-11.

Franklin, J. F., K. Cromack, Jr., W. Denison, A. McKee, C. Maser, J. Sedell, F. Swanson, and G. Juday. 1981. Ecological characteristics of old-growth Douglas-fir forests. PNW-GTR-118. USDA Forest Service, Portland, OR.

Harrison, C. 1978. *A Field Guide to the Nest, Eggs and Nestlings of North American Birds*. Collins, Cleveland, OH.

Harrison, H. H. 1979. *Western Birds' Nests*. Peterson Field Guide Series. Houghton Mifflin, Boston, MA.

Henderson, C. L. 1992. *Woodworking for Wildlife: Homes for Birds and Mammals*. Minnesota Department of Natural Resources, St. Paul, MN.

Hildebrand, D. M. and C. G. Parks. 2002. Inoculation of living trees with stem decay to create cavity nesting habitat. Oregon Chapter of The Wildlife Society Workshop, Feb. 11-12, 2002, Gleneden Beach, OR.

Huss, M. J., J. C. Bednarz, D. M. Juliano, and D. E. Varland. 2002. The efficacy of inoculating fungi into conifer trees to promote cavity excavation by woodpeckers in managed forests in western Washington. In Laudenslayer, W. F., Jr., P. J. Shea, B. E. Valentine, C. P. Weatherspoon, and T. E. Lisle, technical coordinators. 2002. Proceedings of the symposium on the ecology and management of dead wood in western forests. PSW-GTR-181. USDA Forest Service, Albany, CA.

Johnson, V. 1998. Report from Southern Interior Bluebird Trail Society. *Sialia* 20(4):131-132.

Keyser, A. 2002. Western Bluebirds: Life history, population growth, and conservation. *Bluebird* 24(4):10-11.

Kridler, K. 2003. Using feathers to trick and trap House Sparrows. *Bluebird* 25(3):21.

Laubach, R. and C. M. Laubach. 1998. *The Backyard Birdhouse Book: Building Nestboxes and Creating Natural Habitats*. Storey Books, N. Adams, MA.

Link, R. 1999. *Landscaping for Wildlife in the Pacific Northwest*. University of Washington Press in association with Washington Department of Fish and Wildlife, Seattle, WA.

Lundquist, R. W. and J. M. Mariani. 1991. Nesting habitat and abundance of snag-dependent birds in the southern Washington Cascade Range. In Ruggiero, L. F., K. B. Aubry, A. B. Carey, and M. H. Huff, technical coordinators. 1991.Wildlife and vegetation of unmanaged Douglas-fir forests. PNW-GTR-285. USDA Forest Service, Portland, OR.

Marshall, D. B., M. G. Hunter, and A. L. Contreras, editors. 2003. *Birds of Oregon: A General Reference*. Oregon State University Press, Corvallis, OR.

Maser, C., R. F. Tarrant, J. M. Trappe, and J. F. Franklin. 1988. From the forest to the sea: A story of fallen trees. PNW-GTR-229. USDA Forest Service, Portland, OR.

Maser, C. and J. M. Trappe. 1984. The fallen tree – A source of diversity. In Proceedings Soc. of Amer. For. Natl. Conf. October 16-20, 1983, Portland, OR, p. 335-339.

Morse, T. E. 1996. Adaptive strategies of Hooded Mergansers in a Wood Duck world. West Coast Wood Duck Workshop, Feb. 2-3, 1996, Vancouver, WA.

Morse, T. E. and H. M. Wight. 1969. Dump nesting and its effect on production in Wood Ducks. *Journal of Wildlife Management* 33(2):284-293.

Navratil, F. 2002. Letter to the editor. *Bluebird* 24(2):4-5.

Parker, W. J. 2003. My adventures with screech-owls. *Bluebird* 25(1):12-14.

Pearman, M. 2002. *Mountain Bluebird Trail Monitoring Guide*. Red River Naturalists, Red Deer, Alberta.

PNW Forestry Sciences Laboratory. 1993. VHS. Creating cavities in trees: One facet of ecosystem management. USDA Forest Service, Olympia, WA.

Puchy, C. A. and D. B. Marshall. 1993. Oregon Wildlife Diversity Plan 1993-1998. Oregon Department of Fish and Wildlife, Portland, OR.

Rapp V. 2003. New findings about old-growth forests. PNW Science Update No. 4. USDA Forest Service, Portland, OR.

Scott, G. K. 1987. A cheap imitation: How to create nest-cavities. *Birder's World* 1(4):42-45.

Scott, V. E., K. E. Evans, D. R. Patton, and C. P. Stone. 1977. *Cavity-Nesting Birds of North American Forests*. Agriculture Handbook 511. USDA Forest Service, Washington, DC.

Scriven, D. H. 1989. *Bluebirds Trails in the Upper Midwest: A Guide to Successful Trail Management*. Bluebird Recovery Committee of the Audubon Chapter of Minneapolis, Minneapolis, MN.

Shalaway, S. 1995. *A Guide to Bird Homes: Nesting and Roosting Space for Your Backyard Birds*. Bird Watcher's Digest Press, Marietta, OH.

Sharp, B. E. 1997. Avian population trends in the Pacific Northwest. *Bird Populations* 3:26-45.

Sheldon, D. E., Jr. 1998. "Somewhere over the rainbow." *Sialia* 20(4):147-148.

Stanback, M. T. and A. A. Ford. 2002. Bluebirds prefer successful cavities – if they are clean. *Bluebird* 24(2):19-21.

Stokes, D. and L. Stokes. 1990. *The Complete Birdhouse Book: The Easy Guide to Attracting Nesting Birds*. Little, Brown and Company, Boston, MA.

Stokes, D. and L. Stokes. 1994. Tree Swallow behavior. *Bird Watcher's Digest*, Jan./Feb., 1994:94-100.

Strycker, N. 2003. Brown Creepers nest in a manufactured "creeper house." *Oregon Birds* 29(1):17.

Sydeman, W. J. 2002. Of auklets and nest boxes. *Bluebird* 24(4):16-17.

Thomas, J. W., technical editor. 1979. Wildlife habitats in managed forests: the Blue Mountains of Oregon and Washington. Agriculture Handbook No. 553. USDA Forest Service, Washington, DC.

Tuttle, M. D. and D. L. Hensley. 2001. *The Bat House Builder's Handbook*. Bat Conservation International, Austin, TX.

Varland, D. E., R. D. Andrews, and B. L. Ehresman. 1992. Establishing a nest box program for American kestrels along an interstate highway. Iowa Department of Transportation, Ames, IA.

Varland, D. E. and T. M. Loughin. 1993. Reproductive success of American Kestrels nesting along an interstate highway in central Iowa. *Wilson Bull*. 105(3):465-474.

Weston, S. 2001. *Naturescaping: A Landscaping Partnership with Nature*. Oregon Department of Fish and Wildlife, Portland, OR.

Whitworth, T. 2000. Blowflies. *Bluebird* 22(3):14-15.

Winkler, D. W. 1993. Use and importance of feathers as nest lining in tree swallows (Tachycineta bicolor). *The Auk* 110(1):29-36.

Oak Titmouse gathering insects for its nestlings.　LaBelle

INDEX

Ash-throated Flycatcher bringing an insect to feed to its nestlings in a nest box.

ABOUT THE AUTHOR AND PHOTOGRAPHER

Char Corkran studied zoology and paleontology at Brown University, while majoring in American Literature. After moving to Oregon, she was an environmental activist and teacher. Volunteering on wildlife research projects with the Oregon Department of Fish and Wildlife and the Audubon Society of Portland led eventually to a career as an independent wildlife consultant. She co-authored *Amphibians of Oregon, Washington and British Columbia* (1996, Lone Pine Publishing) with Chris Thoms, and has published several articles on wildlife and environmental subjects. Many of her projects have used nest boxes, including Wetland Wildlife Watch, where Bev became a volunteer.

Bev LaBelle studied at the Art Institute of Boston, majoring in photography. Upon graduation she journeyed across the United States photographing landscapes, and ended up settling in the Pacific Northwest. Twenty years ago, she began her love affair with birds, buying her first binoculars and identification book. Soon she was focusing her camera on birds. She recently had a photo essay on Anna's Hummingbirds published in *Oregon Birds*.